God and the Universe

Creation, Providence, and Judgment

in Relation to Modern Science

P.G. Nelson

God and the Universe:
Creation, Providence, and Judgment in Relation to Modern Science

By Dr. Peter G. Nelson

A publication of

The American Journal of Biblical Biblical Theology
Illuminating God's Word

Hayesville, NC 28904

www.biblicaltheology.com

Copyright © 2020, Dr. Peter G. Nelson

All rights reserved. No part of this book may be reproduced, in any form or by any means, without permission in writing from the publisher.

Printed in the United States of America

ISBN: 9798620856626 (Paperback)

Rights for publishing this book in other languages are contracted by the American Journal of Biblical Theology. The AJBT also provides publishing and technical assistance to international publishers dedicated to producing biblically based books in the languages of the world. For additional information, visit www.biblicaltheology.com or write to The American Journal of Biblical Theology, 41 Skid Strip Ln., Hayesville NC 28904 USA, or send an Email to editor@biblicaltheology.com.

Cover photograph by Mark Schulte

CONTENTS

1 Introduction	Page 5
PART I: CREATION	7
2 Reconciling Genesis and Modern Science: A New Approach	9
3 Why Evil? Genesis 1–3 as a Theodicy	15
PART II: GOD'S CONTROL OVER THE UNIVERSE	31
4 Providence and Judgment in Relation to Modern Science	33
5 God's Sovereignty and Human Freedom	61
6 Prayer	79
7 What the Book of Job Teaches about Suffering	87
PART III: RELATED ISSUES	99
8 Demon-possession	101
9 Another Look at the Genesis Flood	105
10 What Will Happen in the End Times	121
EPILOGUE	125

CHAPTER 1

Introduction

This book is about the tension there is between the modern scientific picture of the universe and the Biblical one. On the standard scientific picture, the universe started in a 'Big Bang' – the explosion of a speck of highly concentrated matter 14 billion years ago. According to the Bible, God created the universe in six days about ten thousand years ago. On the scientific picture, the universe has evolved and continues to develop under the operation of fixed laws and chance. According to the Bible, God acts in the universe in providence and judgment, human beings are responsible for their actions, and the Devil plays a part too.

In this book, I seek to resolve these tensions. In Chapter 2, I sketch a new way of reconciling Genesis and modern science based on my book, *Big Bang, Small Voice*.[1] In this I take Genesis 1–3 to be a theodicy (an explanation of how there can be evil in a universe created by a good God). I explain this in more detail in Chapter 3. In Chapter 4, I discuss how God can act in providence and judgment, and human beings can be responsible for their actions, in a universe as described by modern science. This is based on my book, *God's Control over the Universe*.[2] Following on from this, I discuss the whole question of God's sovereignty and human freedom (Chap. 5), the problem of unanswered prayer (Chap. 6), and what the book of Job teaches us

---

[1] P.G. Nelson, *Big Bang, Small Voice: Reconciling Genesis and Modern Science*, 2nd edn. (Hull: Botanic Christian Books, 2014) [available on Amazon].
[2] P.G. Nelson, *God's Control over the Universe: Providence and Judgment in Relation to Modern Science*, 2nd edn. (Latheronwheel, Caithness: Whittles Publishing, 2000) [out of print].

about suffering (Chap. 7). Finally, I consider three related issues: the phenomenon of demon-possession (Chap. 8), scientific evidence for the Genesis flood (Chap. 9), and what will happen in the end times (Chap. 10). I have adapted Chapters 2, 5, and 6 from chapters in my book *Biblical Light on Contemporary Issues*.[3]

To make the discussion accessible to as wide a readership as possible, I shall keep the use of technical language to a minimum. When I do use a technical term, I shall explain what it means. I shall avoid detailed technical discussion but will nevertheless endeavour to be rigorous. Most of the references are to books or articles written at a popular or semi-popular level. Each chapter can be read independently of other chapters. This means that there is some repetition, but I have kept this as low as possible. Except where otherwise stated, I have translated Biblical texts as literally as idiom will allow.

I use the usual abbreviations. LXX refers to the Septuagint, the ancient Greek translation of the Old Testament.

I would like to thank my Christian friends who have been praying for me while I have been working on this book, and the *American Journal of Biblical Theology* for publishing it.

---

[3] P.G. Nelson, *Biblical Light on Contemporary Issues* (Hayesville: AJBT, 2018).

PART I
CREATION

CHAPTER 2

Reconciling Genesis and Modern Science: A New Approach

There are deep divisions among Evangelicals today over Creation. Some ('evolutionists') fully accept the scientific account of origins (Big Bang and evolution), and interpret the Bible according to this.[4] Some ('six-day creationists') take the Biblical account literally, and interpret scientific data according to this.[5] Some ('progressive creationists') take the appearance of 'intelligent design' in organisms to indicate that God specially created these at the points at which they appear in earth history.[6] All three positions have their problems. For example, evolutionists have to take 'death' in Genesis 2–3 to be only spiritual; six-day creationists have to argue that the ages of rocks given by radiometric methods are all completely wrong;[7] and progressive creationists have to explain why God should specially create animals that kill and eat other animals. As Gwyn Jordan argues in a recent letter to *Science & Faith*, there is a great need for Evangelicals to produce a better way of reconciling Genesis and modern science.[8]

---

[4] See, e.g., Denis R. Alexander, *Creation or Evolution: Do We Have To Choose?* (Oxford/Grand Rapids: Monarch, 2008).

[5] See, e.g., Paul A. Garner, *The New Creationism* (Darlington: Evangelical Press, 2009).

[6] See, e.g., William A. Dembski, *Intelligent Design: The Bridge between Science and Theology* (Downers Grove, Illinois: InterVarsity Press, 1999).

[7] The suggestion that radiometric dates are invalidated by a burst of radioactive decay a few thousand years ago (Garner, *New Creationism*, 97–104) is unlikely because of the large amounts of heat and radiation this would have produced.

[8] Gwyn Jordan, *Faith & Thought*, No. 58 (2015) 51–2.

Here I outline two possible ways of doing this, and bring them together.[9]

Preliminaries

I shall assume that the scientific account, subject to the assumptions on which it is based, is broadly correct. I am not saying that it *is* correct. The evidence for this is patchy.

I shall take Genesis 1–3 to be authoritative (Mat. 19:4–6), with Chapter 1 describing the creation of the universe, Chapter 2 the creation of the first man and woman (amplifying 1:26–27), and Chapter 3 their disobedience and punishment.

I shall further take these chapters to constitute a *theodicy*, i.e. an explanation of how there can be evil in a world created by God.[10] Chapter 1 affirms that there was no evil in the world when God created it – it was 'very good' (v. 31). Chapters 2 and 3 explain how evil came into it – through creatures (Adam, Eve, and the Snake) abusing the freedom God had given them. He punished them for this, and changed the natural order to make their lives less pleasant for them. In particular, he cursed the ground, and brought physical death on human beings (cf. Rom. 5:12–21, 8:18–23).

Genesis does not say whether animals died before the Fall.[11] I shall suppose that they did not, but my treatment can be adapted if they did.

First method

I first take Genesis 1–3 figuratively (I take it literally in the second method).[12] I do this on the basis of the Biblical principle that God calls us to live by faith and not by sight (2 Cor. 5:7). He accordingly reveals himself sufficiently clearly for faith to be possible, but not so clearly as to make faith easy. This principle is evident, for

---

[9] For further details, see my book, *Big Bang, Small Voice*.
[10] See Chapter 3.
[11] The definite articles in the Greek of Romans 5:12 may limit the scope of this verse.
[12] *Big Bang, Small Voice*, Part II.

example, in the puzzling visions Daniel had (to test whether he would 'set his heart to understand', Dan. 10:12), and in Jesus' use of parables ('that seeing they may not see, and hearing they may not understand', Luke 8:9–10). If God created the universe in the way scientists describe, and had revealed this in Genesis, then scientists would be able to verify this account, and remove the need for faith. Making Genesis figurative ensures that it would always be a matter of faith that 'the worlds were formed by the word of God' (Heb. 11:3).

If, then, the scientific account of the origin of the universe is correct, Genesis 1–3 teaches, firstly, that *God* (the God of the Hebrews) created it. He designed it and brought it into being. In particular, he chose the laws according to which it operates, the configuration of the components in the Big Bang, and the sequencing of what are to us random events (cf. Prov. 16:33).[13] In other words, he determined how the universe evolved.[14]

Genesis 1–3 teaches, secondly, that, before God brought the universe into being, he changed its design. On his first design, everything was 'very good'. However, he foresaw that human beings would disobey him, just as he foresaw that he would have to send his Son to rescue them (Eph. 1:4). He accordingly changed the design to make the world less pleasant for them, and brought the universe into being in this form.

According to this design, death is part of nature. God's reaction to the disobedience of human beings is seen everywhere. Such is the seriousness of sin.

God created the first modern humans, either by pre-programmed mutations in archaic humans, or by special creation, with a constitution that fits in with the natural order. Genesis 2 teaches how he wants men and women to relate to each other (Mat. 19:4–6, Eph. 5:22–33, 1 Tim. 2:11–15).

---

[13] See further Chapter 4.
[14] The same applies on alternative scientific theories of the universe (Chap. 4).

Second method

In my second method of reconciling Genesis and modern science, I relax two of the basic assumptions of the latter.[15] These are (1) that there is continuous correspondence between theory and reality, and (2) that the natural order is fixed. Relaxing these assumptions allows Genesis 1–3 to be taken literally without pre-empting faith.[16]

Genesis 1 then describes the creation of the universe in six days. At the end of the sixth day, it was a going concern – next morning, the sun rose, plants grew, animals fed. It was, in other words, in a mature state. It accordingly appeared to have a history that it did not in reality have – trees had rings, pebbles were smooth, stars shone at night (despite the length of time it takes for starlight to reach the earth), and so on.

While the concept of a mature creation breaks assumption (1), it does not conflict with science. Any system that runs in an orderly way inevitably appears to have a history when it is set in motion, unless it is from a special state. A pendulum, for example, when set swinging, looks as if it has always been swinging. Not even God can create a mature universe without the appearance of age.[17]

Genesis 3 describes the disobedience of Adam and Eve, as a result of which [contrary to assumption (2)] God modified the design of the universe to make the world less pleasant for them. If he carried this through consistently, so that all parts of the universe conformed to the new design, then the universe would again have been in a mature state, and would again have appeared to have a history it did not in reality have. This history would necessarily have been different from the one it appeared to have before the Fall.

---

[15] *Big Bang, Small Voice*, Part III.
[16] Some details may be figurative, e.g. the description of the sky as a *rāqîaʻ* (1:6–8) if this means '*solid* expanse' (cf. Job 37:18). Compare our 'sunrise' and 'cloudburst'.
[17] For a full discussion, including answers to criticisms of the idea of a mature creation, see my article, 'Another look at mature creation,' *Faith & Thought*, No. 49 (2010), 22–9.

To see what this means for fossils, let us suppose that, on the original design of the universe, only simple organisms and plants died. The original creation, being in a mature state, would therefore have contained fossils of these. Otherwise, it would not have conformed fully to its original design.

On the same supposition, when God redesigned the natural order after the Fall, he brought into it the death of animals, along with predation and disease. To be consistent with this new design, he accordingly refashioned the rocks, and incorporated fossils of animals, including predators and sick specimens. He had to do this to make the cursed earth conform fully to the new design. Otherwise, the biosphere would have conformed to one design and the lithosphere to another. God will make similar radical changes when Jesus comes again (1 Cor. 15:51–52, Rev. 21:1).

Examining the rocks, scientists conclude that animal species evolved over a long period of time. If their analysis is correct, this relates to the cursed design of the universe, and accurately reflects this. It does not, however, relate to the original design, and only represents the actual history of the earth back to the Fall.

Most scientists are unaware of assumptions (1) and (2). Their account of the origin of the universe does, however, depend on them.

According to Genesis 2, God created Adam from dust from the ground and Eve from one of his ribs. After the Fall, they became mortal. In this condition, they correspond to the first fully modern humans in the scientific picture. The evolutionary origin of human beings is a work in progress. Scientists currently believe that modern humans evolved 150,000 to 200,000 years ago, in Africa, from a small population of archaic humans.[18] They do not envisage the small population to be a couple, but the uncertainties in their methodology do not rule this out.

---

[18] See Antoine Suarez, 'Can we give up the origin of humanity from a primal couple without giving up the teaching of original sin and atonement?' *Science & Christian Belief* 27 (2015), 59–83.

If the genealogies in Genesis are complete, the Hebrew version of the text dates creation to around 4000 BC. This is difficult to fit into archaeological history, and suggests that the genealogies are incomplete.[19] Genealogies that gave a verifiable date for the first humans would, in any case, pre-empt faith. There are examples of incomplete genealogies in the Bible, though not with ages at the birth of sons.

Conclusions

That Genesis and modern science can be reconciled in the ways I have described eases the tension between them. There is no need to distort one to make it fit the other. We do not have to contend, for example, that 'death' in Genesis 2–3 is only spiritual, or that the ages of rocks given by radiometric methods are all completely wrong. Rather, we can appraise evolutionary and anti-evolutionary ideas on their merits and ask non-Christians to do the same.

That there is more than one method of reconciliation means that we do not know precisely how God created the universe – whether in a programmed Big Bang or a mature state. This is not as unsatisfactory as it may seem. If, as we study nature and the Bible, we find ourselves groping, this is no bad thing. There is no greater need in the modern world than for men and women to humble themselves before God. 'The fear of the LORD,' says Proverbs, 'is the beginning of wisdom' (9:10).

As Christians, we should not feel ourselves to be under pressure to have answers to *all* the questions people ask. Our message to the world is that God has spoken, not that he has told us everything. Moses referred to God's 'secret things' (Deut. 29:29), and Paul to our seeing 'through a glass, darkly' (1 Cor. 13:12 AV).[20] We need not be ashamed of what we do not know. Our humble 'not knowing' glorifies God as much as our thankful 'knowing'.

---

[19] See Chapter 9.
[20] Gk. *di' esoptrou in ainigmati*, lit. 'through/by a mirror, in a riddle'.

CHAPTER 3
Why Evil? Genesis 1–3 as a Theodicy

One way of understanding Genesis 1–3 is as an explanation of how there can be evil in a world created by God. Genesis 1 affirms that there was no evil in the world when God created it – it was 'very good' (1:31). Genesis 2 and 3 express how evil came into it – through creatures abusing the freedom God had given them. God allowed them to commit their crimes, and only intervened after they had done so (3:8). He then punished them for what they had done, and changed the natural order to make their lives less pleasant for them (3:14–24). In particular, he cursed the ground, and brought physical death on human beings.

This understanding of Genesis 1–3 underlies Milton's *Paradise Lost*. It has, however, been criticized by modern authors.[21] Here I offer a defence of it.

In what follows, Genesis 1' = 1:1–2:3 and Genesis 2' = 2:4–25. I refer to Adam and Eve's disobedience as the Fall and God's response to this as the Curse (the word used in 3:14 and 17).[22]

---

[21] E.g., R.J. Berry, 'This cursed earth: is "the Fall" credible?' *Science and Christian Belief* 11 (1999), 29–49; John J. Bimson, 'Reconsidering a "cosmic fall",' *ibid.* 18 (2006), 63–81; Denis R. Alexander, *Creation or Evolution: Do We Have To Choose?* (Oxford and Grand Rapids: Monarch, 2008), Chaps. 9–13. See also R.J. Berry and T.A. Noble (eds.), *Darwin, Creation and the Fall* (Nottingham: Apollos, 2009); John Polkinghorne, 'Scripture and an evolving creation,' *Science and Christian Belief* 21 (2009), 163–73.

[22] Heb. *'ārar*, opposite of *bārûk̲*, 'bless' (Gen. 12:3).

Relation between Genesis 1' and 2'

Many commentators argue that there are discrepancies between the accounts of creation in Genesis 1' and 2', and that Genesis 2' is from a different source (J) to Genesis 1' (P),[23] or describes the creation of a different race of human beings from Genesis 1'.[24] However, it is possible to harmonize the accounts, such that Genesis 2' amplifies day 6 of Genesis 1', as described below.

Name for God

In Genesis 2', God is called by the personal name *yhwh* ('Yahweh')[25] and title *ʾelōhîm* ('God'), whereas in Genesis 1', he is simply called *ʾelōhîm*. However, in Genesis 2' the narrative becomes more personal. Genesis 1' is about the creation of the universe; Genesis 2'–4 is about the beginnings of human history, starting from two named individuals, Adam and Eve. The introduction of the personal name *yhwh* is therefore explicable.[26]

Function of 2:4

Some scholars take the first half of 2:4 ('These are the generations of the heavens and the earth when they were created') as a concluding summary of Genesis 1', and the second half ('in the day the

---

[23] E.g., John Skinner, *A Critical and Exegetical Commentary on Genesis*, 2nd edn., International Critical Commentary (Edinburgh: T. and T. Clark, 1930).

[24] E.g., E.K. Victor Pearce, *Who Was Adam?*, 2nd edn. (Exeter: Paternoster, 1976), 3rd edn. (Walkerville, South Africa: Africa Centre for World Mission, 1987); Dick Fischer, *The Origins Solution* (Lima, Ohio: Fairway Press, 1996); Berry, 'This cursed earth'; Peter Rüst, 'Early humans, Adam, and inspiration,' *Perspectives on Science and Christian Faith* 59 (2007), 182–93; Alexander, *Creation or Evolution*, Chaps. 9–10. See also R.J. Berry, 'Adam or Adamah?', *Science and Christian Belief* 23 (2011), 23–48.

[25] Meaning 'He is', usually substituted by 'the LORD'.

[26] For a full critique of the documentary hypothesis, see Derek Kidner, *Genesis* (London: Tyndale, 1967), 16–22, 97–100, 184–6, 200–3. See also C. John Collins, *Genesis 1–4* (Phillipsburg, New Jersey: P & R Publishing, 2006), Chap. 8; Richard S. Hess, *Israelite Religions* (Grand Rapids: Baker / Nottingham: Apollos, 2007), 46–59.

LORD God made earth and heavens') as the beginning of a quite separate narrative. Derek Kidner, however, argues that the phrase, 'These are the generations of (*tôl^edôt*)', is a heading, as elsewhere in Genesis.[27] He understands the phrase to mean that those about to be described (Adam, Eve, and the Snake) *issued from* 'the heavens and the earth when they were created', i.e. 'the bare world' of 1:1. Gordon Wenham further argues that 2:4 has a chiastic structure linking the two narratives,[28] though this kind of structure difficult to identify with certainty.

Order of creation of animals and human beings

According to Genesis 1', God made the birds on day 5 (1:20–23) and the land animals on day 6 (1:24–25), followed by human beings (1:26–31). According to Genesis 2', as usually translated, he made a man first (2:7), and then the land animals and birds (2:19). However, this inconsistency can be removed by translating 2:19 as a pluperfect, 'Now the LORD God *had* formed from the ground every animal of the field in addition to every bird of the heavens'. Hebrew verbs do not indicate the time of an action: this is determined by idiom and context. The construction here is unusual for a pluperfect,[29] but other examples are known.[30]

Order of creation of plants and human beings

Genesis 2:5–6 ('... no shrub of the countryside was yet on the earth, and no plant of the countryside had yet sprung up, for ... there was no man to till the ground') could be taken to mean that, when God

---

[27] Kidner, *Genesis*, 23–4, 59.
[28] Gordon J. Wenham, *Genesis 1–15*, Word Biblical Commentary (Waco, Texas: Word Books, 1987), 55. See also Collins, *Genesis 1–4*, 40–2.
[29] S.R. Driver, *A Treatise on the Use of the Tenses in Hebrew*, 3rd edn. (Oxford University Press, 1892), Sect. 76, *Obs*.
[30] C. John Collins, 'The *wayyiqtol* as "pluperfect": when and why,' *Tyndale Bulletin* 46 (1995), 117–40. See also Bruce K. Waltke and M. O'Connor, *An Introduction to Biblical Hebrew Syntax* (Winona Lake: Eisenbrauns, 1990), Sect. 33.2.3; Christo H.J. van der Merwe, Jackie A. Naudé, and Jan H. Kroeze, *A Biblical Hebrew Reference Grammar* (Sheffield: Sheffield Academic Press, 1999), 167–8.

created the first man (2:7), there was no vegetation. This contradicts Genesis 1', where God created vegetation on day 3 (1:11–13) and human beings on day 6 (1:26–31). However, the state of the earth described in 2:5–6 ('… the LORD God had not sent rain on the earth … but a stream[31] went up from the earth and watered all the face of the ground') corresponds to the one presented in 1:2, before God separated the waters (1:6–8) and made the dry land (1:9–10).[32] On this reading, 2:5–6 reminds the reader of the state of the earth when God started creating (2:4), and 2:7 picks up the account of creation on day 6. There is a similar recapitulation at 5:1–2.

Number of human beings created

As usually translated, Genesis 1:26–28 seems to speak of the creation of many human beings ('God said, "Let us make man in our image …, and let them rule …." So God created man in his image …'). This impression goes against Genesis 2', which describes the creation of one man (2:7), and from him, one woman (2:21–22). However, there is a significant change from 1:26 to 1:27. In 1:26, *'ādām* is anarthrous and followed by a plural ("Let us make *'ādām* …, and let *them* …"). In 1:27, on the other hand, *'ādām* has the definite article and is followed by a singular and then a plural ('God created *hā'ādām* in his image, in the image of God he created *him*, male and female he created *them*'). Scholars explain the article as referring back to 1:26 ('the [said] *'ādām*') or as emphasizing *'ādām* ('the [very] *'ādām*') or as a collective ('the *'ādām* [kind]'), and the singular as an effective plural.[33] Later in Genesis, *hā'ādām* is used in a collective sense followed by a singular

---

[31] Heb. *'ēd*, LXX *pēgē*.
[32] Cf. Kidner, *Genesis*, 59–60.
[33] G.J. Spurrell, *Notes on the Text of the Book of Genesis*, 2nd edn. (Oxford: Clarendon Press, 1896), 16; Skinner, *Genesis*, 33; Richard S. Hess, 'Splitting the Adam: the usage of *'ādām* in Genesis i–v,' in *Studies in the Pentateuch* (ed. J.A. Emerton; Leiden: Brill, 1990), 1–15; John D. Currid, *A Study Commentary on Genesis*, Vol. 1 (Darlington: Evangelical Press, 2003), 86–7; Peter Rüst, 'First man versus Adam in Genesis,' *Perspectives on Science and Christian Faith* 60 (2008), 206–7.

(6:5, 8:21). But why should the writer use a singular in 1:27 when he has just used a plural in 1:26?

In a recent study, Paul Niskanen argues that *'ādām* here has both a singular and a collective sense, and that the singular pronoun picks up the former and the plural pronoun the latter.[34] This leads him to suggest the meaning: 'So *ᵉlōhîm* created *hā'ādām* in his image / In the image of *ᵉlōhîm* he created each one'.

A much simpler explanation is that *hā'ādām* means 'the man' as it does in 2:7ff.[35] The switch from singular to plural in 1:27 then correlates with the account in Genesis 2', and allows the plurals in 1:26–28 to be identified with Adam and Eve. There is a similar switch in 5:1–2.[36]

That Genesis 2'–4 amplifies day 6 of Genesis 1' is further supported by the linking of the two passages in 5:1–3 (5:1b–2 summarizes 1:26–28, 5:3 summarizes 4:25). Jesus himself tied 2:24 to 1:27 in Matthew 19:4–5: 'Have you not read that, from the beginning, the Creator "made them male and female", and said, "For this reason a man shall leave his father and his mother, and shall cleave to his wife …"'. Note that Jesus identifies the narrator of Genesis 2' as God himself.

Note finally that Adam named his wife Eve (*ḥawwâ*), 'because she was the mother of all living (*ḥay*)' (3:20). This makes Eve the mother of all humanity, not just of one line of it.

---

[34] Paul Niskanen, 'The poetics of Adam,' *Journal of Biblical Literature* 128 (2009), 417–36.

[35] Cf. LXX (*ton anthrōpon*); Henri Blocher, *In the Beginning* (tr. David G. Preston; Leicester and Downers Grove: Inter-varsity Press, 1984), 55. The article in 2:7 is retained (except after *lᵉ*) until 4:25. From this point, *'ādām* is used as a proper name, and *hā'ādām* has a collective sense. On the use of the article, see Gesenius' *Hebrew Grammar*, 2nd English edn. (ed. E. Kautzsch; tr. A.E. Cowley; Oxford: Clarendon Press, 1910), Sect. 126. See also van der Merwe *et al.*, *Biblical Hebrew Reference Grammar*, Sect. 24.4; Waltke and O'Connor, *Biblical Hebrew Syntax*, Chap. 13.

[36] Here *'ādām* can be taken as a proper name, as in 4:25 and 5:3–5 (cf. LXX).

Nature of the Curse

Many modern scholars interpret the Curse in relational terms.[37] They understand 'Let us make man in our own image' (1:26) to mean that God created human beings with the capability of having a relationship with him. They go on to infer that Adam and Eve had such a relationship, and that the main effect of the Curse was the breaking of this. The Curse also adversely affected Adam and Eve's relationship with each other, and with the natural world.

Scholars support this interpretation by pointing out that God told Adam that, 'on the day' that he ate from the tree of the knowledge of good and evil, he would die (2:17). Since on the day that he did eat from it, he did not die physically, the reference must be to 'spiritual' death, i.e. to being cut off from God.[38]

Scholars also point out that God told Eve, 'Your urge will be to your husband,[39] but he shall rule over you' (3:16b). He also told the Snake, 'I will put enmity between you and the woman, and between your offspring and her offspring ...' (3:15). These punishments are relational.

Scholars further note that God also told Eve, 'I will greatly multiply your painful toil[40] ...' (3:16a), and infer from this that there was suffering before the Curse.

This scheme of interpretation leaves the natural order largely unchanged. Only the relationship of human beings with it has changed. There were thorns and thistles before the Curse, but only after the Curse did they become a nuisance to human beings (3:17–19). This means that what we call 'natural evils' (predation, disease, earthquakes, etc.)

---

[37] E.g., Berry, 'This cursed earth'; Bimson, 'Reconsidering a "cosmic fall"'; Alexander, *Creation or Evolution*, Chaps. 11–13. See also Collins, *Genesis 1–4*, Chap. 6; Berry, 'Adam or Adamah?'.
[38] See, e.g., Berry, 'This cursed earth'; Alexander, *Creation or Evolution*, Chap. 11. See also Berry, 'Adam or Adamah?'.
[39] Compare 4:7 where the same idiom is used.
[40] Heb. *'iṣṣābôn*, as in 3:17 and 5:29.

existed before the Curse, and are not evils. In God's eye's, they are 'very good' in the sense that they are part of a creation that is fit for the purpose for which he created it.[41]

There are several problems with this approach as I discuss below.

Image of God

There must be considerable doubt whether the ancient Hebrews understood 'image of God' (ṣelem ʾelōhîm)[42] to imply 'capable of having a relationship with God'. They are more likely to have taken it to mean 'looking like God and representing him', as the context in Genesis implies ('Let us make man in our image, according to our likeness, and let them rule over [the earth]', 1:26).[43] Remember that, when Ezekiel saw 'the appearance of the likeness of the glory of the LORD', he saw 'a likeness with the appearance of a man' (Ezek. 1:26–28). Note also that, in the New Testament, Paul says that a man should not cover his head in worship because he is the 'image and glory' of God (1 Cor. 11:7). In any case, in the narrative, not only do Adam and Eve have a relationship with God, so does the Serpent. God speaks to him, as he does to Adam and Eve.

The terms 'image' and 'likeness' are used in a similar way in 5:3. Here Seth is described as being the likeness and image of Adam. What does this mean but that Seth looked like his father and represented him? Adam's other sons are not so described (4:1–2, 5:4).

Death

Genesis defines the death imposed on Adam in two ways. First, God says to him, 'dust you are, and to dust you shall return' (3:19).

---

[41] Ernest Lucas, 'God and "natural evil"', *Faith and Thought* No. 50 (2011), 16–26. Cf. Robert S. White, *Who Is To Blame? Disasters, Nature, and Acts of God* (Oxford/Grand Rapids: Monarch, 2014); Christopher Southgate, *Theology in a Suffering World: Glory and Longing* (Cambridge University Press, 2018).

[42] The Hebrew requires us to look for a more concrete meaning than the Latin *imago Dei*.

[43] Cf. Kidner, *Genesis*, 51; Richard S. Hess, 'Genesis 1–2 and recent studies of ancient texts,' *Science and Christian Belief.* 7 (1995), 141–9.

This describes physical death. Second, the narrator states that God drove Adam away from the tree of life lest he should eat from it and 'live for ever' (3:22–24). This means that he would cease to live (5:5), in contrast to what happened to Enoch (5:24). The reference again is to physical death.

What about God's warning to Adam that he would die 'on the day' he ate from the tree of the knowledge of good and evil (2:17)? Genesis presents the fulfilment of this in 3:17–19 and 22–24: on the day Adam ate from this tree, God pronounced death on him, and drove him away from the tree whose fruit would have given him immortality. In other words, he changed Adam's life from one that would not lead to physical death to one that did.

It is true that New Testament scholars distinguish between 'physical death' and 'spiritual death'. This does not mean, however, that Genesis 2'–3 is only about spiritual death.[44] In any case, the distinction is not as clear in the New Testament as is commonly supposed. For example, when Jesus says that a person who exercises faith in him 'has gone over from death to the life' (John 5:24), he could be referring to a change in *regime*, from one (lit. 'the death') that leads to physical death and hell to one ('the life') that takes a person through physical death into heaven (cf. Mat. 7:13–14; John 3:36, 6:47, 8:51, 11:25–26; 1 John 3:14).

Similarly, when Paul says in Romans 7 that he 'died' when faced with the Law (vv. 9–10), this could mean that, like Adam, he became *subject* to death. In Cranfield's words,[45]

---

[44] Cf. Leon Morris, 'Death,' *New Bible Dictionary*, 301–2. Morris points out that 'the Scriptural passages which connect sin and death do not qualify death. We would not understand from them that something other than the usual meaning attached to the word.' Compare also Philip Duce, 'Comment on "This cursed earth"', *Science and Christian Belief* 11 (1999), 159–65.

[45] C.E.B. Cranfield, *The Epistle to the Romans*, International Critical Commentary, Vol. I (Edinburgh: T. and T. Clark, 1975), 352.

Though he continues to live, he is dead – being under God's sentence of death (cf. v. 24b). Physical death, when it comes, is but the fulfilment of the sentence already passed.

In the previous chapter, Paul speaks of two 'ends', death and eternal life (6:21–23).[46]

A key verse is 5:12, where he says, (lit.) 'as through one human being the sin entered into the world, and through the sin the death, and so the death spread to all human beings, in that all sinned.' Here he is evidently referring to God's pronouncement of death on Adam and eviction of him from the Garden of Eden, which brought death, and denied access to the tree of life, not only to Adam, but also his posterity.[47] The reference is therefore to physical death.[48]

The only distinction that the New Testament makes explicitly is between 'death' and 'second death'. The latter refers to the death of the wicked following their resurrection from the first death (Rev. 20:11–15, 21:8). It is again a bodily death.

In a recent book, John Walton reasons that, since Adam's immortality depended on him eating from the tree of life, he was, by nature, mortal.[49] Berry takes this as supporting his contention that Adam's punishment was only spiritual.[50] Allaway endorses Walton's reasoning.[51] However, the angry tone of God's pronouncement of death in 3:17–19 ('dust you [are] and to dust you shall return!') points to this entailing a more radical change in Adam's constitution than would be the case if he was by nature mortal and nature simply took its course. A better reading is to take Adam as having been created immortal, and the function of the tree of life broadened from conferring everlasting

---

[46] See further P.G. Nelson, *Science and Christian Belief* 12 (2000), 166–7; *Making Sense of Romans* (Seaford: Thankful Books, 2009), 41–2, 44.
[47] *Making Sense of Romans*, 36.
[48] Whether 'the death' includes the death of animals depends on how the article is understood. I discuss the death of animals in *Big Bang, Small Voice*, 51–3.
[49] John H. Walton, *The Lost World of Genesis One* (Downers Grove: IVP, 2009), 98–100.
[50] 'Adam or Adamah?', n. 65.
[51] Bob Allaway, *Faith and Thought* No. 60 (2016) 32–3.

life on mortals (3:22) to *signifying* and *confirming* everlasting life to immortals.[52]

Punishment of Eve

God's punishment of Eve was almost certainly more physical than relationalists infer. When God said to Eve, 'I will greatly multiply your painful toil ...' (3:16a), this does not necessarily mean that Eve was suffering already. The verb (*rābâ*) does not always denote multiplication.[53] It can simply mean 'make great'. The sense is then, 'I will make very great your painful toil ...'. Before the Curse, nerve impulses in Adam and Eve could have been sufficiently strong to act as a warning but not so strong as to cause suffering.

To 'painful toil', God adds 'conception':[54] 'I will make very great your painful toil and your conception'. Puzzled by this, commentators treat 'painful toil and conception' as a hendiadys, meaning 'pain in childbirth'. But a high level of conception makes sense. Eve would need to have more children to compensate for the physical death of human beings.[55]

God's punishment of the Snake was also partly physical as I discuss further below.

Sequel

In the narrative, Adam and Eve *continue to have a relationship with God* after the Fall (4:1), as do their sons, Cain and Abel (4:3–7). The first reference to someone being cut off from God is when Cain murders Abel and is banished from Eden (4:8–12). Fearing that

---

[52] Cf. Gordon J. Wenham, *Genesis 1–15* (Waco, Texas: Word Books, 1987), 62; Collins, *Genesis 1–4*, 115, 160–2; *Did Adam and Eve Really Exist?* (Nottingham: Inter-Varsity Press, 2011), 62, 65–6, 115–6. See my letter in *Faith and Thought* No. 62 (2017), 44–5.
[53] Blocher, *In the Beginning*, 180–1 and n. 16.
[54] Heb. *hērôn*.
[55] Cf. Carol Meyers, *Discovering Eve* (New York and Oxford: Oxford University Press, 1988), Chap.5. She links the increase in conception to the labour of growing food outside the garden.

someone from Abel's family might find him and kill him, Cain protests, 'My punishment is greater than I can bear. Look, you have driven me away today from the face of the ground, and I shall be hidden from your face …' (4:13–14). After God ensures that no one will kill him, we read that 'Cain went out from the presence of [lit. "from before"] the LORD …' (4:15–16).

Curse of the ground

God says to Adam, 'cursed is the ground because of you' (3:17). He does not say, 'cursed are you in relation to the ground' (cf. Deut. 28:20). The ground is not the whole of nature, but it affects a large part of it.

Goodness of the creation

There are two major problems with taking what we call 'natural evils' (predation, disease, earthquakes, etc.) to be 'very good'. The first is that later Biblical writers do not regard them as 'very good'.[56]

For example, the prophet Isaiah foresaw that, in the reign of the Messiah, 'the wolf shall live with the lamb, … and the lion shall eat straw like the ox' (Isa. 11:6–7). However metaphorical this passage may be, Isaiah is making a clear value judgment in it. This is that the state of a wolf living with a lamb or of a lion eating straw is better than the state of a wolf tearing a lamb apart or a lion eating flesh. The latter cannot therefore be 'very good'.

Exponents of a relational Curse answer this by pointing out that there are passages in the Bible praising God for creating and feeding predatory animals (e.g. Psa. 104).[57] However, God is no less Creator and Sustainer of the cursed earth as he was of the uncursed. Jesus spoke of God making the sun to rise on the evil as well as the good (Mat. 5:45).

---

[56] *Big Bang, Small Voice*, 50–2.
[57] See, e.g., Bimson, 'Reconsidering a "cosmic" fall.'

In any case, Genesis clearly implies that there was no predation before the Curse. In 1:29–30, God says to the first human beings, 'Behold, I have given to you every plant yielding seed that is on the face of all the earth, and every tree yielding seed in its fruit. It shall be food for you. And to every animal of the earth, and every bird of the heavens, and every creeping organism on the earth, all the greenery of plants is for food' (cf. 9:3–4).

This passage presents a serious problem to relationalists. To his credit, Denis Alexander tries to address this.[58] He writes, 'It is unlikely that this text refers to vegetarianism, more likely that it is highlighting the theological point that animal sacrifice was necessary only for those who had sinned.' However, this is unconvincing. For God not to say in Genesis 1 that animals can eat other animals because human beings before the Fall did not need to offer sacrifices is very contrived.

Alexander goes on to say that 9:3–4 represents 'the renewal of God's covenant to Noah in which he expressly mandates the eating of all animals, except for their blood'. However, the wording does not indicate a renewal of 1:29–30 but a development of it: 'Every moving thing that is alive shall be food for you; like the greenery of plants, I have given you everything.' The comparison, 'like (k^e) the greenery of plants', points to an extension in what can be eaten. Early Jewish commentators understood these texts in this way:[59]

> R. Jose b. R. Abin said in R. Joḥanan's name: Adam, to whom flesh to satisfy his appetite was not permitted, was not admonished against eating a limb torn from a living animal. But the children of Noah, to whom flesh to satisfy their appetite was permitted, were admonished against eating a limb torn from a living animal [Exod. 22:31].

John Collins tries to downplay 1:29–30 by saying that, while this passage states that man and animals were given plants to eat, 'it does

---

[58] Alexander, *Creation or Evolution*, 271–2.
[59] *Midrash Rabbah, Genesis* 34.13 (Soncino translation).

not say that they ate nothing else'.⁶⁰ The inference that some were carnivorous, besides being forced, takes no account of 9:3–4.

Some scholars maintain that the changes required to convert a herbivore into a carnivore are too big for this transformation to be possible. The changes are surely not, however, too big for God.

Ernest Lucas has recently argued that, on the traditional understanding of Genesis 1–2, Adam and Eve would have been like pampered pets.⁶¹ However, this underplays the moral challenge posed by the command not to eat from the tree of the knowledge of good and evil. Indeed, this challenge was sufficiently strong for Adam and Eve to fail. Lucas says that his motivation for reinterpreting Genesis is to take account of 'what, after some careful investigation, seem to be valid scientific conclusions about the age of the earth, its history and the history of life on earth'. However, it is possible to reconcile Genesis and modern science without abandoning the traditional interpretation of the former or distorting the latter as I indicate at the end.

The second problem with taking the natural world as we know it to be 'very good' is that the psalmist wrote of the earth and the heavens 'wearing out' and one day being 'changed' (Psa. 102:25–26). Isaiah prophesied that God will create 'new heavens and a new earth' (Isa. 65:17–25). Jesus alluded to this prophesy when he spoke about 'the regeneration' (Mat. 19:28). Peter urged Christians to look for its fulfilment (2 Pet. 3:1–13). John was given a vision of it happening (Rev. 21:1–22:5). This strand of Bible teaching implies that the heavens and the earth themselves, in their present state, are less than 'very good'. Indeed, the last passage contains the statements, 'there shall be no longer be death, or mourning, or crying, and no longer be pain' (21:4), and *'there shall no longer be any curse'* (Rev. 22:3), relating back explicitly to Genesis 3.

---

⁶⁰ *Genesis 1–4*, 165.
⁶¹ 'God and "natural evil"'.

Jesus himself treated 'natural evils' as bad. He healed disabilities and diseases (Mat. 4:23–24 etc.), and warned his disciples about decay and natural disasters (Mat. 6:19–20, 24:7, etc.). He linked the collapse of a tower and congenital blindness to the general sinfulness of human beings, not the particular sins of those concerned (Luke 13:4–5, John 9:1–3a). He thus took them as arising out of a natural order that is as it is because of the general sinfulness of humankind – the order after the Fall.

These considerations settle the meaning of other Biblical passages on the creation. Thus, when Ecclesiastes speaks about the futility of the natural order (1:1–11), he links this to the mortality of human beings (vv. 4, 11), which renders even good aspects of nature futile (vv. 5–7). He is evidently therefore referring to the creation in its cursed state. Likewise, when Paul describes the creation as having been subjected to futility, he links this to the present human condition (Rom. 8:18–23). His picture of the whole creation groaning and travailing together, waiting to be freed from the bondage of corruption, points forward to the promise of a new heaven and a new earth, and no more curse.

The Snake[62]

Most commentators take the Snake to be, or to symbolize, or to be in thrall to, the Devil. This confounds the theodicy.

However, there is nothing in the passage to indicate this.[63] The author refers to the Snake throughout by the ordinary word for snake (*nāḥāš*), and describes him as one of the animals God had made (3:1). The author nowhere states that he is inherently evil, only 'clever' (*'ārûm*, 3:1), a word that can have a good or bad sense (e.g. Prov. 12:16 and Job 5:12 respectively). What the Snake does is misuse its cleverness with the very reasonable argument that eating from the tree of the knowledge of good and evil would not bring death, only

---

[62] Traditionally rendered 'Serpent', but this has mythical associations.
[63] Cf. Victor P. Hamilton, *The Book of Genesis Chapters 1–17*, New International Commentary on the Old Testament (Grand Rapids: Eerdmans, 1990), 187–8.

knowledge of good and evil (3:1–5). After God curses him, he becomes the animal we know, living on its belly, eating at ground level, menacing and being menaced by human beings (3:14–15).

It is true that, in the New Testament, the Snake *is* identified with the Devil (Rev. 12:9, 20:2). If Genesis 3 is understood literally, this means that the Serpent, having started off as one of the animals, *became* the Devil. Its spirit lived on after the death of its body, attaching itself to the angels, and marauding the earth (Job 1:6–7, 2:1–2; 1 Pet. 5:8, etc.). Its physical offspring, however, are the snakes we know (cf. Luke 10:18–19).

Many Christian commentators identify the Devil as a fallen angel, who posed as, or took possession of, the Snake. This identification is based on Isaiah 14:12–15 and Ezekiel 28:13–17. However, the first prophecy concerns the king of Babylon (Isa. 14:4) and the second the king of Tyre (Ezek. 28:12).[64] The identification in any case misses the whole point of Genesis 3, that evil in the world originated *within* it, and did not come in from outside. God created the world good; creatures misused their freedom and spoilt it.

Conclusion

There is a good case for taking Genesis 1–3 as a theodicy. When people ask, 'Why do natural disasters happen?', we can answer, 'When God created the universe, it was good; when human beings disobeyed, he made the world a less pleasant place.' There is no need to look for an explanation elsewhere.

This understanding of Genesis constrains the way we seek to reconcile the Biblical account of creation with modern science. There are still methods of doing this, however. Donald MacKay has presented one,[65] and I have given two others.[66]

---

[64] Blocher, *In the Beginning*, 42.
[65] Donald M. MacKay, 'The sovereignty of God in the natural world,' *Scottish Journal of Theology* 21 (1968), 13–26.
[66] See Chapter 2.

PART II
GOD'S CONTROL OVER THE UNIVERSE

CHAPTER 4

Providence and Judgment in Relation to Modern Science

According to the Bible, God is actively involved in the world, in providence and judgment; the Devil is actively involved too. According to modern science, however, the universe is evolving according to fixed laws, and under the operations of chance; day-to-day events are either predetermined or happen accidentally. Moreover, human beings are not fundamentally different from other animals, whereas in the Bible, they are responsible to God for their actions. The tension between these two pictures is widely felt. It not only contributes significantly to the doubts of unbelievers but is also a problem for many Christians.

In this chapter, I want to show that the Biblical and the scientific picture of the world do not conflict with each other as much as they might appear. In particular, I want to show that, even if the scientist's perception of the world is fully accepted, mechanisms still exist by which God can control the world in whatever way he wants to, and human beings can take actions for which they are responsible.

To facilitate my presentation of this, I shall take the two components of the scientific picture (determinism and chance) and deal with these in turn. I will then discuss the agency of human beings, and how God can control a world containing them. I will also consider briefly the agency of the Devil.

Several other writers have addressed the question of science and providence in recent years. I compare their treatments with mine at appropriate points in the text.

1 God's control over a universe that scientists would describe as completely determined

In this section, I shall suppose that the universe is like a huge machine, i.e. that it comprises a large number of elementary parts whose behaviour is completely determined by simple, fixed laws. This is how scientists pictured it in the 18th and 19th centuries. More recently, scientists have introduced chance into the picture, but they still regard many of the workings of the universe as being completely determined, e.g. when calculating the thrusts required to get a satellite into orbit.

God's control over a completely mechanical universe is twofold: *creative* and *final*.

Creative control

God can control the history of a completely mechanical universe in the choices he makes when he creates it. These choices fall into two groups.

Constitution

First of all, God has a choice of what the components of the universe will be, and of what laws will determine their behaviour. This choice determines the general character of the universe.

According to some cosmologists, even a slight change in the laws of physics would have produced a universe that is quite different from our own. They speak as if the laws have to be finely tuned to produce a universe in which human beings can exist (the so-called 'anthropic principle').[67] However, other cosmologists have questioned this, arguing, for example, that there could be an underlying law which fixes

---

[67] P.C.W. Davies, *The Accidental Universe* (Cambridge University Press, 1982); *The Goldilocks Enigma* (London: Allen Lane, 2006); John D. Barrow and Frank J. Tipler, *The Anthropic Cosmological Principle* (Oxford University Press, 1986); John Gribbin and Martin Rees, *Cosmic Coincidences* (London: Black Swann, 1991); Geraint F. Lewis and Luke A. Barnes, *A Fortunate Universe: Life in a Finely Tuned Cosmos* (Cambridge University Press, 2016).

the relationship between the presently known ones.[68] Whether this is so or not must be left an open question. What is certain, however, is that, of all the possible laws or sets of laws God could have chosen, only for some would the universe be hospitable to human beings, and only for one would it be exactly as it is.

Initial conditions

In addition to having a choice over the components and the laws, God also has a choice over the arrangement of the components when he sets the universe in motion.[69] This determines the particular history of the universe. One arrangement leads to one sequence of events (e.g. a solar flare on 1st January 2100), another to another (no solar flare). God chooses the history he wants by arranging the components accordingly.

This choice gives God a very precise control over the history of the universe. The number of ways of arranging the parts of a mechanical system at the point at which it is set in motion is, in general, very great. Furthermore, each arrangement leads, in general, to a different motion. Indeed, studies have shown that the motion of complex mechanical systems is extremely sensitive to the choice of initial conditions – even only a very slightly different set of conditions can lead to a completely different motion.[70] Thus which of the possible motions a mechanical system executes is very precisely determined by the particular set of starting conditions that are chosen for it.

A mechanical universe is therefore very complicated. The laws may be simple: remarkably so. But the complexity that is possible on the basis of these laws is enormous. That God should be able to command this complexity is a measure of his deity.

---

[68] Steven Weinberg, *Dreams of a Final Theory* (London: Hutchinson Radius, 1993).
[69] I am presupposing that there is an absolute time scale for the universe. Such a scale can be established from astronomical measurements on distant galaxies [Jayant V. Narlikar, *The Primeval Universe* (Oxford University Press, 1988), 53–6].
[70] I discuss this further in Section 3.

An analogy

The two kinds of creative control God has over a mechanical universe are illustrated by *Life*, a program devised by the mathematician John Conway.[71] When run on a PC, the screen is divided into cells, and the operator is invited to darken some of the cells to produce a pattern. The program takes the pattern and converts into another according to a set of simple rules. It then converts the second pattern into a third and so on to produce a moving picture on the screen.

Like the history of a mechanical universe, the moving picture on the screen depends on two choices. The first is the set of rules; the second is the starting pattern. For each set of rules, there is a very large number of starting patterns, each of which produces a different drama on the screen. To obtain one particular drama, the starting pattern has to be chosen accordingly.

Initial state on different models of the universe

On the big bang model, there is a natural initial state – the singularity from which the universe expands. Cosmologists have, however, proposed models of the universe that do not have a natural initial state.[72] On these, the history of the universe either extends backwards in time indefinitely, or else repeats itself in cycles.

There is, however, an essential difference between a mathematical model of the universe, and the universe itself.[73] For a universe to exist, it has to be brought into being. This is something God can do at any time. When he does, the universe will, if it is not in a natural initial state, appear to have a history that it does not in reality have – just as a pendulum that has been set swinging appears always to have been swinging.[74]

---

[71] See, e.g., William Poundstone, *The Recursive Universe* (Oxford University Press, 1987).
[72] See, e.g., P.C.W. Davies, *Space and Time in the Modern Universe* (Cambridge University Press, 1977), Sect. 6.4.
[73] Cf. Stephen W. Hawking, *A Brief History of Time* (London: Bantam, 1988), 174.
[74] Cf. Chapter 2.

Organizational laws

In recent years, some scientists have questioned the generally accepted scientific picture of the universe, feeling that it does not explain the degree of organization that there is in it, especially in living organisms.[75] They suggest that there may be laws governing the behaviour of a composite system that are distinct from, but compatible with, the laws governing the motion of its parts. They describe the effect of the former as 'top-down' causation, as opposed to 'bottom-up' causation produced by the latter.

This suggestion does not affect God's control over the universe, since, if there are organizational laws, he has chosen them. Note, however, that, in a completely mechanical universe, the origin of any such laws may lie in the arrangement of components at the beginning. If these form a pattern, this pattern will propagate as the universe evolves.

Certainly, the behaviour of a complex mechanical system can only be fully understood when it is treated as a whole. When its motion is reduced to that of its constituent parts, an essential feature is lost – the relationship between the parts. Reduction is a useful tactic in science, but a false strategy.

Final control

God has one other means of control over a completely mechanical universe. He can change it or bring it to an end. It is his creation; he can do with it what he wills.

In the meantime, he 'sustains' the universe in the sense that he keeps it in being as it is.

---

[75] See, e.g., Paul C.W. Davies, *The Cosmic Blueprint* (London: Heinemann, 1987). Cf. Arthur Peacocke, *God and the New Biology* (London: Dent, 1986); *Theology for a Scientific Age*, 2nd edn. (London: SCM Press, 1993).

2 God's control over a universe that scientists would describe as undetermined

Chance in science

When someone tosses a coin, the outcome is completely outside his or her control. Because of this it is customary to attribute the result to chance.

However, the fact that the outcome is outside the person's control does not mean that it is undetermined. In a completely mechanical universe, the whole process is determined, and if one could measure the impulses on the coin, one could calculate its motion and predict how it would land. The outcome is thus indeterminate to the person, not absolutely.

Scientists believe that many natural phenomena are indeterminate in this sense, i.e. are completely determined in principle, but indeterminate in practice.[76] Examples are the motion of a branch in a gusty wind, turbulent flow in a fast-moving stream, and unstable weather patterns. Models of these systems can be constructed on which the behaviour is completely determined, but what happens is so sensitive to the initial state as to make the accuracy with which this has to be specified much greater than any scientific measurement can achieve.

Some scientists argue from this that phenomena of this type are *un*determined,[77] but this does not follow.[78] Indeed, many scientists describe the chaotic behaviour displayed by such systems as 'deterministic chaos'. Phenomena of this type do not therefore affect

---

[76] See, e.g., Davies, *Cosmic Blueprint*, Chap. 4; James Gleick, *Chaos* (New York: Viking, 1987); David Ruelle, *Chance and Chaos* (Princeton University Press, 1991).

[77] Ilya Prigogine, *From Being to Becoming* (San Francisco: Freeman, 1980), 43–4 (but compare next note); John Polkinghorne, *Reason and Reality* (London: SPCK, 1991), Chap. 3. Polkinghorne bases his theodicy on this view.

[78] Cf. Ilya Prigogine and Isabelle Stengers, *Order out of Chaos* (Toronto: Bantam, 1984), 271–2; Ian Stewart, *Does God Play Dice?* (Oxford: Blackwell, 1989), 303.

God's control over the universe, which remains as I described in Section 1.

There are other natural phenomena, however, which have led scientists to develop theories in which indeterminism and chance appear in a more deep-seated way. These theories bring in chance in relation to (1) multiple or recurrent events, (2) single events.

Multiple or recurrent events

Chance is involved in connection with two of the basic theories of modern physics, quantum mechanics and statistical mechanics. Quantum mechanics is concerned with the motion of microscopic objects, statistical mechanics with the way in which these motions give rise to the properties of macroscopic objects. Both are statistical theories, giving only average results.

How chance is involved in connection with these theories is best seen by means of examples.

Quantum theory. Consider a beam of light passing through two pieces of Polaroid. When these are at 45°, nearly half of the photons that pass through the first piece pass through the second. This result is correctly predicted by the quantum theory. However, the theory arrives at this result without considering what happens to individual photons. It is only able to predict the proportion of photons that will get through, not what will happen in individual cases. This is like predicting that a coin will land with its head uppermost 50% of the times it is tossed, without being able to predict (as one cannot without detailed information) what will be the outcome of any particular toss.

Statistical mechanics. Consider a gas in an isolated container. Scientists have found that, if they make the assumption that the motion of the molecules in the gas is completely random, they can calculate the properties of the gas with great precision. For example, they can deduce that the gas exerts the same pressure in all directions, as is observed experimentally (e.g. in the shape taken up by a bubble). The calculations involve considering the motion of the system of molecules taken as a whole. This motion is continually changing because of external influences.[79] Let the number of possible motions of the system having an energy equal to the energy of the gas be n. Then completely random means that, over the course of a long period of time, all of the n possible motions occur, and do so with the same frequency ($= 1/n$). This is again similar to tossing a coin for which $n = 2$.

From our introductory discussion, the apparent randomness in the motion of microscopic particles suggests two possibilities:

(1) there exists a more exact theory than the quantum theory and statistical mechanics, which will account for the motions of microscopic particles in the same way that an exact mechanical treatment of coin-tossing would account for the sequence of heads and tails that came up in a series of throws; or
(2) the motion of microscopic particles is fundamentally indeterminate.

On the choice between (1) and (2) there has long been a debate in physics. Some scientists (e.g. Bohr) have argued that the behaviour of microscopic systems is such that no more exact theory is possible: nature is fundamentally indeterminate. Others (e.g. Einstein) have resisted this conclusion (as Einstein put it, 'God does not play dice'). Present opinion is divided.[80] I shall leave the question open, as no-one can be sure how science will develop in the future.

Scientists who adopt view (2) attribute the outcome of an individual microscopic event to 'chance'. For some this is simply another way of saying that the outcome of such an event cannot be predicted from its circumstances – it has no immediate cause. Others

---

[79] For a full discussion, see K.G. Denbigh and J.S. Denbigh, *Entropy in Relation to Incomplete Knowledge* (Cambridge University Press, 1985), Sect. 2.3 and App. 2.2.
[80] See, e.g., P.C.W. Davies and J.R. Brown (eds.) *The Ghost in the Atom* (Cambridge University Press, 1986).

use the word 'chance' to mean than an event has no ultimate cause.[81] This usage goes beyond science.[82]

Single events

Chance is invoked in relation to single events, both in science and in everyday life. These are events for which the outcome is, or seems to be, only one of number that could have occurred.

Monod divided events of this kind into two categories:[83]

(1) *Coincidences*. These are incidents that result from the intersection of what appear to be two completely independent chains of events. Monod gives the example of a carpenter working on a roof dropping his hammer on someone who happens to be walking underneath.

(2) *Inherently unpredictable events*. These are events whose outcome is rendered uncertain by the indeterminacy in microscopic processes described in the previous section. Monod gives as an example a mutation of a gene. According to the quantum theory, when a gene is subjected to a perturbation (e.g. collision with a high-energy particle) various outcomes are possible, and all that can be predicted is the probability of a particular result.

God's control of 'chance' events

In this section, I shall discuss God's control over 'chance' events in the categories I have just described. In doing so, I shall picture the universe as being completely determined as Einstein believed or fundamentally indeterminate as Bohr maintained.

---

[81] Jacques Monod, *Chance and Necessity* (tr. Austryn Wainhouse; London: Collins, 1972); P.W. Atkins, *The Creation* (Oxford: Freeman, 1981) and other books; Richard Dawkins, *The Blind Watchmaker* (Harlow: Longman, 1986) and other books.
[82] Cf. Donald M. MacKay, *Science, Chance, and Providence* (Oxford University Press, 1978), Chap. 2.
[83] *Chance and Necessity*, 110–2.

Multiple or recurrent events

As we have seen, when a scientist attributes a series of events to chance, he or she is taking the fact that they form a similar pattern to that obtained by repeatedly tossing a coin, and applying the same description as is used in the latter case. However, the fact that a series of events forms a random pattern does not necessarily imply lack of control. Consider, for example, a lawn that has been sown by hand. If the gardener has sown it well, the seeds will appear to be randomly distributed over the plot, with each square decimetre containing a similar number of seeds. But this distribution will not have come about purely by chance. It will be what the gardener set out to achieve when he sowed the plot.

Another example is provided by the random numbers that are used in science and for other purposes. These are generated by a random-number program in a computer. To users, these numbers are completely random. However, they are produced by a quite definite mathematical procedure.[84] To a mathematician or a computer programmer, they are as determined as numbers produced by any other mathematical procedure.

Thus, the fact that some natural events conform to a random pattern does not mean that God has no control over them. He has both the means to control them and a purpose for them.

Means of control

If the universe is completely determined (Einstein's view), God can control events that form a random pattern by the way he sets the component parts going at the beginning (Sect. 1). He can introduce some degree of dispersion into their motions to start with. This dispersion will then propagate as the universe develops.

If, on the other hand, the universe is fundamentally indeterminate (Bohr's view), God can decree the outcome of events individually, in

---

[84] Davies, *Cosmic Blueprint*, 74–5.

such a way as to secure an apparently random distribution overall. One way he can achieve this is by using a sequence of random numbers, and making the outcomes follow this sequence. This is what scientists do when simulating random processes in nature, e.g. radioactive decay.[85] (Random-number programs are deterministic, remember.)

Whichever mechanism God uses, his control is perfect. The fact that science can only describe a series of events statistically does not mean that God cannot determine them. What is indeterminate to us is not indeterminate to him.[86]

Purpose

Apparently random series of events constitute an essential part of the design of the universe. For a gas to have the properties it has, it is necessary that the sequence of motions of the molecules comprising it should include all (or most) possibilities and form an even distribution. For example, if the molecules in the earth's atmosphere, instead of moving in all directions, all moved in the same direction (say from east to west), they would generate a continual high wind that would make human life on earth impossible. God's glory is in no way diminished by apparent randomness in the universe: he employs this feature to secure the kind of universe he wants.

A second example concerns mutations. Most biologists believe that these are random in the sense that they are not determined by whether or not they are advantageous to an organism in its environment.[87] If this is correct, then the randomness provides a mechanism whereby an organism can adapt to a change in environment. If all mutations had the same effect, they would not help

---

[85] See, e.g., John D. McGervey, *Quantum Mechanics* (San Diego: Academic Press, 1995), Fig. 14.2.
[86] Cf. Prigogine and Stengers, *Order out of Chaos*, 272: 'if [God] made use of his absolute knowledge, then he could get rid of all randomness'. I here follow MacKay, *Science, Chance, and Providence*, Chap. 2. I depart from David J. Bartholomew, *God of Chance* (London: SCM Press, 1984); John Polkinghorne, *Science and Providence* (London: SPCK, 1989) and other books; and Peacocke, *Theology for a Scientific Age*.
[87] Cf. Dawkins, *Blind Watchmaker*, 306–12.

an organism in a new environment, unless they happened to be beneficial. But if the mutations are random, then, while most will not help the organism, some may.

Single events

God can control single events in the same way as described in the previous section. A Biblical example is when someone seeks his guidance by casting a lot (e.g. Josh. 18–19, Acts 1:15–26). According to Proverbs, 'The lot is cast into the lap, but its every decision is from the LORD' (16:33).

Beginning of the universe

Some scientists speculate that the big bang arose from a quantum fluctuation in the vacuum of space and attribute this to chance.[88] This again goes beyond science. To attribute the beginning of the universe to chance is no more rational or scientific than to attribute it to God.

Some scientists have suggested that there might be an infinite number of universes, either existing separately, or as different regions of a 'multiverse'.[89] A random distribution of laws and initial conditions among these universes would then generate the universe we inhabit without having to invoke divine choice. However, this rests on a very large assumption (that there is an infinite number of universes) and still requires a choice to be made – that of a random distribution.

---

[88] E.g. Atkins, *The Creation*.
[89] See, e.g., John Leslie, *Universes* (London: Routledge, 1989); David Layzer, *Cosmogenesis* (Oxford University Press, 1990); David Deutsch, *The Fabric of Reality* (London: Allen Lane, 1997); Stephen Hawking and Leonard Mlodinow, *The Grand Design* (London: Bantam, 2010).

3 Human agency

Free will

The question of whether or not human beings have free will (i.e. the power to determine whether or not to do something) is vigorously debated, both by philosophers and theologians. I shall assume that, within certain bounds, they do, based on the following considerations.

Firstly, my experience as a human being is of being faced with alternative courses of action, and having to choose between them. While experiments apparently show that subjects make simple test decisions subconsciously some time *before* they are aware of making them consciously,[90] I doubt whether this is true of decisions that have to be thought through carefully.[91]

Secondly, the Bible teaches that human beings are responsible to God for their actions. The Old Testament states that God will render to everyone according to his or her deeds (Psa. 62:12, Prov. 24:12, etc.). The New Testament, while presenting a way by which sinners can be forgiven, affirms this (Mat. 13:47–50, 16:24–27, 25:31–46, etc.). Paul explained how people are culpable for their actions even when they do not know God's law (Rom. 2:14–16). James insisted that no-one can blame God if he or she sins (Jas. 1:13–15). I take the view that, if human beings are responsible for their actions, they must be free to determine these actions.[92] Otherwise, they *could* blame God when they sin.

I shall assume, then, that human beings do have free will in this full sense,[93] and give myself the task of explaining how God can control

---

[90] Benjamin Libet, *Mind Time: the Temporal Factor of Consciousness* (Harvard University Press, 2004); C.S. Soon, A.H. He, S. Bode, and J.-D. Haynes, 'Predicting free choices for abstract intentions,' *Proceedings of the National Academy of Sciences of the USA* 110 (2013), 6217–22.

[91] Cf. Alfred R. Mele, *Effective Intentions: the Power of Conscious Will* (Oxford University Press, 2009); Peter G.H. Clarke, 'Neuroscientific and psychological attacks on the efficacy of conscious will', *Science and Christian Belief* 26 (2014), 5–23.

[92] Cf. Ecclesiasticus 15:11–20.

[93] Philosophers describe this kind of free will as 'incompatibilist' because it is incompatible with a completely determined universe. They also speak about

the world in this circumstance. On the alternative assumption that human beings are bound by their constitution and environment to perform the acts they do, God's control over the universe is unaffected by the presence of human beings, and remains as I described in Sections 1 and 2.

Scientific basis for human freedom

Many scientists have considered how it might be possible for human beings to have freedom of action if the universe is as described by modern science. I have reviewed their various suggestions elsewhere.[94] Here I present my own proposal, based on Polkinghorne's idea that free ill is associated with bifurcation points in the working of the brain.[95]

Suppose that I have to decide between two courses of action, A and B. Suppose further that my brain, body, and environment comprise a physical system, made up of components interacting and moving according to fixed laws. Then the sequence of thoughts that I have in making my decision corresponds to a series of configurations of the physical components of my brain.

Suppose now that a superscientist is able to observe these configurations and predict from the laws of physics how they will change. Two results are possible. The first is that the superscientist correctly predicts what I will choose. In this case, the thoughts encoded on my brain must follow a sequence that is determined equivalently by their content and the laws of physics. Thus, if my thoughts lead to 'I will do A', the physics of my brain must lead to the configuration corresponding to 'I will do A'.

This must certainly be what happens when I carry out an arithmetic calculation. In this case, my thoughts must follow the logic

---

'compatibilist' free will, but however this is conceived, it fails the test I have just applied, i.e. it does not make human beings answerable for their actions [cf. P. van Inwagen, *An Essay on Free Will* (Oxford University Press, 1983)].

[94] 'Freewill in a deterministic universe,' *Faith and Thought* No. 44 (2008), 21–6.
[95] Polkinghorne, *Science and Providence*.

of the method that I use, and the configuration of my brain must follow a sequence corresponding to this, established when I learned the method.[96]

The second possibility is that the superscientist predicts that the assembly of physical components in my brain reaches a bifurcation point between two configurations, one corresponding to 'I will do A' and the other to 'I will do B'. A quantum-mechanical calculation gives a 50% probability of the assembly proceeding to the first configuration and 50% to the second.

How then do I make my decision? The answer is, I suggest, that *my thoughts themselves* determine the outcome at this point. As we have seen, when I make a predictable decision, my thoughts follow a sequence that is determined equivalently by their content and the laws of physics. At a bifurcation point, however, the physics is undetermined. In this case, the outcome must be determined by the content of my thoughts alone. In other words, *I* make the decision, and am answerable to God for it.

Origin of mechanism

If this mechanism is essentially correct (the details are doubtless more complicated), its origin can be explained as follows.

As a child grows, its brain develops by cells multiplying and differentiating according to the child's genes, and by the whole structure interacting, through the nerves and sensory organs, with the rest of the body and the outside world. This leads eventually to activity among the neurons that the young person experiences as an awareness of having to think about and make a decision. So far, this is, in the young person, a bottom-up process, determined by physics and chemistry.[97]

---

[96] Cf. Nancey Murphy, 'The problem of mental causation: how does reason get its grip on the brain?', *Science and Christian Belief* 14 (2002), 143–57.
[97] Outside influences from parents and other adults may be top-down.

Once this point has been reached, a top-down process becomes possible. This is when the young person's consideration of the options facing him or her gives rise to a bifurcation point in the brain. In this circumstance, the young person's thoughts themselves, by proceeding along one line rather than another, determine the direction the brain takes. This then constitutes a free choice.

If this is correct, then God either created human beings with brains that are capable of encoding thoughts that can drive the brain, or so designed the primordial universe to evolve human beings with brains having this capability.

4 God's control over a universe containing human beings

God has three means of control over a universe containing human beings with free will in the full sense discussed in the previous section. Two of these are the same as those I described in Sections 1 and 2, one is additional.

Creative control

God's creative control over the universe is necessarily reduced by the presence of other agents. If men and women are free to make choices, then the choices they make will play a part in determining the history of the world.

However, since human beings are God's creatures, their ability to determine events is something God has chosen to give them. He wanted them to be able to act freely, and designed them in such a way that they can do so, as we saw in Section 3.

Moreover, he placed bounds on their freedom. By giving them the physical and mental capacity that they have, and placing them in the environment that they are in, he determined their scope and limitations – what they can and cannot do.

God's creative control over a universe containing human beings thus consists of his determination of a *set* of possible histories, with each history depending on the choices human beings make, and each choice circumscribed by the limits he has set. Some events are common to all possible histories, e.g. sunrise and sunset over London on 1st January 2100. Other events vary from history to history, e.g. the weather over London on this day, since this depends on, among other things, how much carbonaceous fuel human beings decide to burn in all the years before. The actual history within all the possible histories is determined by men and women themselves.

God's creative control may thus be likened to the control a landowner has who decides to convert some of his land into orchards and let them to a tenant. By his choice of land, how he drains it, what trees he plants in it, the buildings he erects, the terms of the tenancy, and whom he lets it to, he determines the possible futures of his property. Within these possible futures, the actual future is determined by the tenant.

This illustration corresponds closely to the account of creation given in Genesis. God creates a garden for Adam and Eve (2:8–9) and leaves them to look after it. Compare also the beginning of Jesus's parable of the tenants: 'There was a certain landowner who planted a vineyard, set a hedge around it, dug a winepress in it, and built a watchtower. He then leased it to vine-dressers and went into a far country …' (Mat. 21:33–44).

God's ability to determine possible histories of the world means that he can determine the consequences of the choices human beings make. He can, for example, make obeying his laws carry pleasant consequences, and disobeying them unpleasant ones, either in the short term or the long term (cf. Gal. 6:7–8). The Bible stresses that God gave his laws to his people for their good (Deut. 6:24, etc.): they are maker's instructions.

God's use of foreknowledge in creation

Some theologians go further than I have done above.[98] They suggest that God knows in advance what a human being, acting freely, will do in a particular situation. He therefore knows in advance what the history of a world, containing particular human beings, living through particular situations, will be. He can therefore create a world that has whatever history he chooses, even though the human beings in it are free agents.

However, it is debatable whether human beings have free will in this circumstance.[99] If God knows (with certainty) what they will do in a particular situation, other than by observing them do it, they are bound to do it.[100] I shall make the more difficult assumption that, while God knows what human beings will do in many situations (cf. 1 Sam. 23:10–11, Psa. 139:1–6, John 6:64, etc.), he does not know what they will do in all (cf. Gen. 6:5–7, Luke 13:6–9, etc.). The question is then, how does he nevertheless control the history of the world?

Intervenient control

God has a second means of control that he can exercise in a world containing human agents. This is to override the usual mechanisms that determine events in the world, and make things happen that would not otherwise have happened. He can do this in two ways.

Direct interventions

First, God can intervene directly, i.e. he can break into the natural course of events at the point he wants something different to happen

---

[98] William Lane Craig, *The Only Wise God: The Compatibility of Divine Foreknowledge and Human Freedom* (Grand Rapids: Baker, 1987).

[99] See, e.g., Paul Helm, *The Providence of God* (Leicester: Inter-Varsity Press, 1993), 55–61.

[100] I have added 'other than by observing them do it' to cover the point made by Scott R. Burson and Jerry L. Walls, *C.S. Lewis & Francis Schaeffer* (Downers Grove: InterVarsity Press, 1998), 99. They note that foreknowledge can be obtained by using a time machine. However, foreknowledge obtained in this way cannot be used to change the future.

and change what happens at this point. The Bible records many instances of such interventions. Most are associated with particular phases of Biblical history, particularly the exodus of the Israelites from Egypt and the ministry of Jesus. Examples are when Jesus touched a leper and the leprosy immediately disappeared (Mat. 8:2–3), and when he rebuked a storm on the Sea of Galilee and it stopped straightaway (Mat. 8:23–27).

Events of this kind conflict of course with the scientific picture of the universe. Even on a modern probabilistic view, the probability of their occurrence is so low that scientists would regard them as events that could not happen. It must be remembered, however, that the scientific picture has been built up by considering only the regular features of the universe. For example, Newton discovered the law of gravity by considering the motion of the planets and everyday events on earth; he did not consider the occasion when Jesus walked on water (Mat. 14:25). This is not because he did not believe in the latter, but because he drew a distinction between God's activity in revelation and in nature. The scientific picture is thus by its very nature a partial one; it tells us how the universe functions most of the time, but it does not tell us about God's interventions in it.

How often we can expect God to intervene directly in the world is a difficult question. This is not the place to try to resolve it, except to note the following consideration. God wants human beings to use their freedom in a particular way: he wants them to worship him, trust him, and obey him. For them to be able to do this effectively, he must reveal himself to them; but for them to be able to do this voluntarily, he must also hide himself from them so that they are not forced to do it. God has therefore carefully to measure his interventions so as to make faith possible, but not pre-empt it (cf. Deut. 29:29; Isa. 45:15; Mat. 12:38–40, 13:10–17; John 20:24–29; etc.).

For this reason, God maintains an element of mystery about his activity in the world. Paul professed that, in this life, 'we see through a glass, darkly' (1 Cor. 13:12 AV), and declared, 'O the depth of the riches of the wisdom and knowledge of God! How unsearchable are his judgments, and his ways past finding out!' (Rom. 11:33).

Indirect interventions

As well as being able to intervene directly, God can also intervene indirectly, i.e. he can effect a change at some point further back from the one at which he wants something different to happen, and then allow the natural flow of events from this point to bring it about. This mechanism allows God to intervene more discreetly than the first, and to make greater demands on faith. It also allows him to intervene more frequently.

An example of such an intervention is when Paul was being taken to Rome by boat and a severe storm developed along the coast of Crete, driving the ship into the central Mediterranean (Acts 27). In response to Paul's prayers, God made the boat run aground on the tiny island of Malta. However, he did not do this directly. The storm still raged; the boat still drifted and tossed. No-one could see God doing anything. Yet somehow, he so controlled the storm that Paul was kept safe, and all who sailed with him.

A human illustration of such control is provided by the way finance ministers seek to manage a nation's economy. If, for example, they want people to spend less money, they do not try to stop them spending directly, but make a change at some other point in the economy which they hope will have this effect (e.g. they may reduce taxes on savings). This illustration is of course imperfect – the degree of control finance ministers have over a country's economy is relatively small; nevertheless it does show how it is possible to control an event at one point in a system by taking action at another.

In relating God's indirect interventions to the scientific picture of the universe it must be remembered that the latter is based on a comparatively small number of observations of natural systems. Scientists are quite incapable of keeping track of all the elementary components of the universe, and of showing that the laws of science are adhered to all the time. God can alter a sun spot, change a weather pattern, introduce a new virus, stop a man's heart, stimulate a thought, without scientists knowing that he has done so. This is especially the case for those systems whose motion is extremely sensitive to small changes in conditions as discussed in Section 2.

Thus, by means of interventions, God can control a universe containing human beings as tightly as he wants. He can destroy corrupt cities (Gen. 19:24), arrange for two strangers to meet (Ruth 2:3), stir up a storm (Jon. 1:4), cause a virgin to have a child (Luke 1:26–37), open the heart of a seeker (Acts 16:14), and so on. He can act in providence and judgment.

Non-intervention

Since God chooses when to intervene in the world, he also chooses when not to intervene. In this sense, his non-interventions also form part of his control over the universe. They might be described as 'permissive' control. This control takes two forms.

General non-intervention

As we have seen, God has given human beings freedom in the way that they live and made them responsible for the conduct of their lives. He accordingly limits his interventions in the world, so as to preserve this freedom and maintain this responsibility. Moreover, he continues to do this despite the wickedness of men and women, since to deal with evil in the world would be to prevent believers from growing in faith (Mat. 13:24–30, 36–43) and deny sinners the possibility of repentance (Luke 13:1–9, 2 Pet. 3:9).

God's respect for the freedom God has given to human beings is brought out by the fall of Adam and Eve (Gen. 3). God did not intervene when the serpent began to tempt Eve; he did not go into the garden until after the couple had committed their act of disobedience (v. 8). Compare also the parable of the prodigal son (Luke 15:11–32), in which the father gives the son what he demands (v. 12) and lets him go off (v. 13). Paul speaks of God 'giving up' sinners to the consequences of their sins (Rom. 1:24, 26, 28).

Among the incidents in human life that God allows are what we would describe as tragedies or disasters. When Jesus was asked about these he made it clear that, in general, God does not bring them about in response to the particular sins of the individuals involved, but that they belong to an order in which all have sinned (Luke 13:1–5, John 9:1–3a). At the same time, he spoke of his work in the lives of individuals to bring them to repentance (Luke 13:6–9).

Also, among the incidents God allows are 'chance' ones, in the sense of events that are partly or wholly determined by the action of human beings but are beyond their control. The law of Moses makes provision for homicides of this kind, 'as when a man goes into a forest with his neighbour to cut wood, and his hand makes a stroke with the axe to cut down a tree, and the head slips from the handle and strikes his neighbour so that he dies' (Deut. 19:1–7). This incident is similar to the one described by Monod (Sect. 2). No doubt most games of chance come into this category, e.g. in dice God allows each die to fall in the way each player throws it. Only when there is something particularly at stake might he intervene.

On a positive note, God also allows human beings creative freedom, i.e. the freedom to produce new things out of the material of the universe. These include art and music, as well as buildings, machinery, new plant varieties, and so on. Men and women can abuse this freedom, and often do, but some use it well, especially those who elicit the help of the Holy Spirit.

That God maintains the orderliness of nature to the degree that he does is a mercy (Gen. 8:21–22, Jer. 31:35–36). Human life would be much more difficult without it.

Specific non-interventions

As well as refraining from intervening in the world to maintain human freedom, God can also choose not to intervene for more specific purposes. In particular, he can allow bad things to happen, and use them in a chain of events that leads, in the end, to what he wants. The Bible contains some striking examples of this, e.g. his deliverance of

Israel from famine through the wrong done to Joseph by his brothers (Gen. 37–50). Joseph later told his brothers, 'You intended evil against me, but God meant it for good, to bring about what is being done today, the saving of many lives' (50:20).

God therefore controls the universe by a judicious combination of intervention and non-intervention. As Paul told the Romans, 'God works in all things for the good of those who love him, of those who are called according to his purpose' (Rom. 8:28). God has evidently so designed the universe – so balanced the forces acting within it – that he can to a very large extent allow human beings to do what they want, and the natural order to take the course that human actions determine, while at the same time, by intervening discreetly here and there, carry forward his purpose of calling a people to himself, and working for their ultimate good. Indeed, he can if he wishes bring to pass something he has predestined, fulfil a prophecy that he has inspired, or answer a prayer that he wants to hear, without having to take away human freedom to do it (cf. Acts 2:23, 4:27–28, etc.).

Jesus spoke of God's deployment of both intervention and non-intervention when he prepared his disciples for the dangers that would face them (Mat. 10:16–33). He pointed to the sparrows that were caught, killed, and sold for food, and said, 'not one of them will fall to the ground without your Father' (v. 29). In other words, God only allows a particular bird to be snared at the moment he chooses. Until then, if necessary, he intervenes to prevent it. Jesus's teaching was fulfilled for his disciples, who were both preserved from martyrdom (Acts 5:17–42, 12:3–19) and exposed to it (Acts 6:8–7:60, 12:1–2).

In summary, God permits a great many happenings in the world, some of which he is pleased to see, many of which he is not. He does not *will* the latter to happen, except to the extent that he wills the freedom he has given to human beings and can use their wrongdoings 'for good' (Gen. 50:20, Rom. 8:28). Hence the prayer Jesus taught his disciples to pray, 'Our Father in heaven, … your will be done on earth as it is in heaven' (Mat. 6:9–13).

Some theologians speak of God having two wills, one willing what he would like to happen and the other what actually happens.[101] However, it is one thing to say that God permits evil to happen, and another that he *wills* it to happen, except as a punishment in certain circumstances (Isa. 45:7 etc.).

An illustration

An illustration of how God can control the world while allowing human beings freedom is the way in which a mountain shepherd controls his flock. To get his sheep from one pasture to another, he does not have to tie leads round their necks and pull them along. He can choose a route so that the flock will tend to stay together, he can gently guide the leading animals in the right direction, and he can send his dog to usher an animal back that wanders too far away. He can thereby get his flock to a new pasture while allowing the animals almost complete freedom to go where they want.

This illustration is imperfect, but it does show how God can accomplish his purposes in the world without taking away human freedom. He can let human beings take most of the actions they want to, and only override them (intervene) occasionally. The Bible frequently uses the shepherd and his flock as a picture of God's dealings with his people.

Comparison with other views

My picture of the relationship between God and the world lies between the extreme views, (1) that God has complete control over everything that happens in the world, including every human action,[102] and (2) that, while God acts to influence human beings (e.g. sending his Son), he allows them to have complete control over their own

---

[101] See, e.g., D.A. Carson, *Divine Sovereignty and Human Responsibility* (London: Marshall, Morgan and Scott, 1981), 212–4.

[102] Helm, *Providence*; Melvin Tinker, *Intended for Good: the Providence of God* (Nottingham: Apollos, 2012); Ron Highfield, *The Faithful Creator: Affirming Creation and Providence in an Age of Anxiety* (Nottingham: Apollos, 2015).

actions and to determine their history.[103] On my picture, God allows human beings almost complete freedom of action, while at the same time maintaining effectively complete control over their history.[104] If men and women threaten to do something he does not want to allow, he can intervene to close off this option, or present them with a more attractive one. Alternatively, he can allow them to act, and intervene afterwards to recover his purposes. Only rarely need he override their freedom.

His providence, in other words, is effectively 'risk-free'.[105] Even in the extreme case of early humans behaving so badly that he regretted making them, he was able to recover his purposes by flooding the world and saving Noah (Gen. 6–9).

Salvation

On the thorny question of whether human beings are free to accept the gospel, this study shows that, whichever way we answer this, God is still sovereign. If he wants people to be free to respond, he can allow them this freedom, while still controlling the history of the world in the ways I have described.[106]

---

[103] Clark Pinnock, Richard Rice, John Sanders, William Hasker, and David Basinger, *The Openness of God* (Downers Grove: InterVarsity Press, 1994); John Sanders, *The God Who Risks* (Downers Grove: InterVarsity Press, 1998); Gregory A. Boyd, *God of the Possible: a Biblical Introduction to the Open View of God* (Grand Rapids: Baker, 2000); Clark H. Pinnock, *Most Moved Mover: a Theology of God's Openness* (Carlisle: Paternoster/ Grand Rapids: Baker, 2001). Polkinghorne also presents an 'open' picture of the universe (*Science and Providence* and other books). See also Stanley N. Gundry (ed.), *Four Views on Divine Providence* (Grand Rapids: Zondervan, 2011).

[104] Cf. J.R. Lucas, *Freedom and Grace* (London: SPCK, 1976), 29–30; Peter Geach, *Providence and Evil* (Cambridge University Press, 1977), 57–9. My picture combines theirs, allowing God to exercise tight control (Geach) or loose control (Lucas) as he wills.

[105] Cf. Helm, *Providence*, Chap. 2.

[106] For a full discussion, see Chapter 5.

Re-creative control

Major changes to universe

God can intervene in more radical ways than those described in the preceding section, and change even the working of the universe itself. According to the Bible, he did this at the Fall (Gen. 3), and perhaps also to some degree at the Flood (Gen. 6:5–9:17). The Bible also says that he will do this again in the future, to produce 'a new heaven and a new earth' (Isa. 65:17–25, Rev. 21:1–5). In the meantime, he is gathering a people for himself, and making them, through Christ, 'new creations' (2 Cor. 5:17).

Present state of universe

The world in its present state contains a great deal of suffering. As discussed in Chapter 3, the Bible attributes this to the Curse, God's response to the Fall (Gen. 3).

Paul describes the creation in its present state as being under 'the slavery of corruption', and speaks of it 'groaning and travailing' (Rom. 8:20–23). In this state, human beings become ill, grow old, and die, and tragedies and natural disasters occur, e.g. lands have famines (Gen. 41:53–57, etc.), men and women are born with disabilities (John 9:1, Acts 3:2), buildings collapse on people (Luke 13:4). While God brings some of these things about in response to specific sins (Exod. 7–12, etc.), he mostly allows them to happen because of the general sinfulness of humankind (Luke 13:4–5, John 9:1–3a), or to refine the faith of his people (Rom. 5:1–5, Jas. 1:2–4, 1 Pet.1:6–9, etc.). On a future day, however, the creation will be released from this condition (Rom. 8:19–21); the curse on it will be removed, and a new order established, under the rule of Christ (Isa. 11:1–9, 65:17–25; Rev. 21:1–5, 22:1–5).

God also allows human beings to commit atrocities, again either because of the general sinfulness of humankind (Luke 13:1–3), or to punish particular sins (2 Chr. 36:15–21, etc.), or to refine his people's faith (Zech. 13:7–9, etc.). Daniel was assured, in relation to such happenings: 'many of those who sleep in the dust of the earth shall awake, some to everlasting life, and some to shame [and] everlasting contempt' (Dan. 12:1–3). In the book of Revelation, John sees in heaven believers in Jesus 'who come out of the great tribulation', standing before the throne of God, suffering no more (Rev. 7:9–17).

The universe in its present state therefore displays two things: the power and deity of God (Rom. 1:20), and the seriousness of sin (Gen. 3:17–19, Rom. 8:20–23).

5 Other agents

Biblical writers refer to the Devil and other spiritual beings acting in the universe. The presence of these agents makes God's control over the universe more complicated, but he can still achieve control by the mechanisms I have described.

The Devil

According to the Bible, the Devil began as a snake (Gen. 3:1).[107] He was a free agent (God held him responsible for his actions, Gen. 3:14–15). He abused his freedom, tempting Adam and Eve to sin (Gen. 3:1–7). God punished him for this, making him into the snake we know (Gen 3:14–15). His spirit lives on as the Devil (Rev. 12:9, 20:2).

The Bible teaches that the Devil has considerable influence in the world. Jesus described him as 'the ruler of this world' (John 12:31, etc.), Paul as 'the god of this age' (2 Cor. 4:4). He is capable of bringing trouble on people (Job 1:6–19, 2:1–7; Luke 13:11, 16), i.e. of intervening in the world.

However, God has set bounds to his influence. God created him with limits to his freedom like other creatures (Gen. 3:1). After the Fall God reset these limits (Gen. 3:14–15), and now places specific restrictions on what he can do in relation to individual men and women (Job 1:12, 2:6). He allows the Devil to go so far, but no further.

---

[107] See Chapter 3.

Also, God can intervene to frustrate or reverse the Devil's actions (Job 42:10–17, Rev. 12:15–16). He did this supremely in the ministry of Jesus (Luke 11:14–23), and in Jesus' submission to death on the cross (John 12:31–32). This has made the Devil even more active in the world (Rev. 12), but when God recreates the universe, he will banish the Devil completely from it, casting him a lake of fire (Mat. 25:41, Rev. 20:10).

God allows the Devil to test the faith of his people (Job 1–2, Luke 22:31–32). The message of the book of Job is that not all suffering is a punishment for sin. Job's friends thought that it was (4:1–9 etc.), but God told them that they were wrong (42:7).[108]

---

[108] See Chapter 7.

CHAPTER 5

God's Sovereignty and Human Freedom

The relationship between God's sovereignty and human freedom has long exercised theologians.[109] It divided Pelagius and Augustine, Erasmus and Luther, Arminius and Calvin, Wesley and Whitefield. It divides contemporary Calvinists and 'open' theists. Here I present a systematic treatment of the subject that does justice both to God's sovereignty and to human freedom. I hope that this will help to reconcile different views on the issue.

The problem

What do we mean by 'God's sovereignty' and 'human freedom'? Possible answers are:

(S1) *God's sovereignty*: God determines everything that happens in the universe.

---

[109] There is an extensive literature on this subject. Recent texts include: D.A. Carson, *Divine Sovereignty and Human Responsibility* (London: Marshall, Morgan and Scott, 1981); Clark Pinnock (ed.), *The Grace of God, the Will of Man* (Grand Rapids: Zondervan, 1989); Paul Helm, *The Providence of God* (Leicester: Inter-Varsity Press, 1993); Clark Pinnock *et al.*, *The Openness of God* (Downers Grove: InterVarsity Press, 1994); Thomas R. Schreiner and Bruce A. Ware (eds.), *The Grace of God and the Bondage of the Will* (2 vols.; Grand Rapids: Baker, 1995); Thomas R. Schreiner and Bruce A. Ware (eds.), *Still Sovereign* (Grand Rapids: Baker, 2000); David N. Steele, Curtis C. Thomas and S. Lance Quinn, *The Five Points of Calvinism*, 2nd edn. (Phillipsburg: Presbyterian and Reformed, 2004); Roger E. Olson, *Arminian Theology* (Downers Grove: InterVarsity Press, 2006); John C. Lennox, *Determined To Believe?* (Oxford: Monarch, 2017).

(F1) *Human freedom*: Human beings determine some of the things they do.[110]

As thus defined, God's sovereignty and human freedom are incompatible. There can be sovereignty without freedom, or freedom without sovereignty, but not both.

One way in which philosophers have tried to get round this problem is by redefining human freedom as follows:[111]

(F2) *Human freedom*: Human beings do what they want to do.

As thus defined, human freedom is compatible with a completely determined universe. In such a universe, human beings are still aware of wanting things, even though their wanting is determined.

However, this kind of freedom does not make human beings responsible for their actions. This is because, on the Day of Judgment, they could say to God, '*You* determined the wrong things I did by the way you set up the universe.' James insists, however, that no one can blame God when he or she sins (Jas. 1:13–15; cf. Ecclesiasticus 15:11–20).

Another way in which scholars have tried to resolve the problem is by appealing to one of the basic theories of modern science (the quantum theory).[112] According to one understanding of this, the universe is not completely determined.[113] At a microscopic level, it is undetermined. For example, in a sample of a radioactive substance, the radioactive atoms do not all decay together, but randomly.

However, this picture does not help us. If there are events in the universe that are, to scientists, undetermined, this does not make them

---

[110] This definition allows for 'involuntary' action.
[111] Helm, *Providence*, 67.
[112] See, e.g., A.S. Eddington, *The Nature of the Physical World* (Cambridge University Press, 1928), Chap. 14; Danah Zohar, *The Quantum Self* (London: Bloomsbury, 1990).
[113] See Chapter 4, Section 2.

undetermined to God.[114] God can determine when radioactive atoms decay, whether they decay together, or randomly. In any case, not all scientists believe that the universe is undetermined at a microscopic level.[115] Einstein is one who did not.

A resolution

A more promising suggestion is to say that God uses his sovereignty to give human beings freedom.[116] He certainly has the power to do this – if he wants human beings to have freedom, he can give it to them. This leads to another definition of sovereignty:

> (S2) *God's sovereignty*: God allows human beings to determine some of the things they do, and determines everything else that happens in the universe.

At first sight, this definition is unsatisfactory. If human beings determine some things, it would seem that God can no longer work out his purposes in the world. He can no longer, for example, 'work all things together for good' for those who love him (Rom. 8:28). In other words, his sovereignty would seem to be so severely diminished as to empty the word 'sovereignty' of its meaning.

However, God has many ways of controlling human behaviour without taking away human freedom.[117] In the first place, he has designed human beings and their environment in such a way that, while they can do many things, they cannot do many other things. Secondly, he can intervene in the causal mesh of the universe to change the circumstances in which a human being makes a decision without letting

---

[114] Donald M. MacKay, *Science, Chance and Providence* (Oxford University Press, 1978), Chap. 2.

[115] See, e.g., P.C.W. Davies and J.R. Brown (eds.), *The Ghost in the Atom* (Cambridge University Press, 1986).

[116] See, e.g., Richard Swinburne, *The Coherence of Theism* (Oxford: Clarendon Press, 1977), 175–6.

[117] See Chapter 4, Section 4. Cf. William James, *The Will to Believe and Other Essays in Popular Philosophy* (New York: Longmans, 1897), 180–2; J.R. Lucas, *Freedom and Grace* (London: SPCK, 1976), 29–30; Peter Geach, *Providence and Evil* (Cambridge University Press, 1977), 57–9.

his intervention be known. This is because the universe is a complex and subtle system. Scientists speak of a butterfly in one part of the world affecting the weather in another part.[118] God can make a small change at one point to bring about a significant change at another point.

So, for example, if he sees a man who is thinking of doing something that would obstruct his purposes, he can intervene to close off this option, or present him with a more attractive one. Alternatively, he can allow him to act, and intervene afterwards to recover his purposes. Only rarely need he override the man's freedom.

We can therefore redefine God's sovereignty in a way that is consistent with human freedom as follows:

(S2′) *God's sovereignty*: God controls everything that happens in the universe.

God can control what happens in the universe very tightly or very loosely depending on what he wants to achieve. To secure the death of an evil king in disguise on a battlefield, by a stray arrow that found a gap in the latter's armour, he had to exercise very tight control (1 Kgs. 22:29–38). To 'give up' sinners to their sins (Rom. 1:24, 26), he need only exercise very loose control. Texts that scholars use to prove that world history is 'open' or 'closed' really reflect the different ways God exercises control in it.

Evil

Philosophers have long puzzled over the question of how there can be evil in a world created by a good God.[119] As discussed in Chapter 3, the Bible answers this question in Genesis 1–3. Genesis 1 affirms that there was no evil in the world when God created it – it was 'very good' (1:31). Genesis 2 and 3 explain how evil came into it –

---

[118] See, e.g., James Gleick, *Chaos* (New York: Viking, 1987), 9–31. The effect occurs under unstable weather conditions.

[119] See, e.g., Marilyn McCord Adams and Robert Merrihew Adams (eds.), *The Problem of Evil* (Oxford University Press, 1990); Peter Vardy, *The Puzzle of Evil* (London: Fount, 1992)..

through creatures (Adam, Eve, and the Snake) abusing the freedom God had given them. God allowed them to commit their crimes, and only intervened after they had done so (3:8). He then punished them for what they had done, and changed the natural order to make their lives less pleasant for them (3:14–24). In particular, he cursed the ground, and brought death on human beings.

This answer to the problem of evil corresponds to the 'free will defence' of philosophers.[120] My earlier discussion shows that this defence does not mean that God has no control over the world. He has all the control he wants.

Genesis 3 describes the natural order as it now is, scarred with suffering and death. These will not be present in the 'new heaven and new earth', but they are an inextricable part of the world now. God does not take them away, even for Christians, except in special circumstances. Jesus forewarned his disciples, 'In the world you shall have tribulation' (John 16:33).

Genesis 3 also describes the Snake, now the Devil,[121] as having some influence in the world. God evidently allows him to have this, while at the same time keeping his activity in check. The Devil's freedom is a paradigm of human freedom: he has it, but cannot prevent God from achieving his purposes.

Salvation

We now come to the thorny questions:

(1) Are people free to accept or reject the gospel?
(2) If they are free to accept it, can they do so without God's help?

---

[120] See, e.g., Alvin Plantinga, *God, Freedom and Evil* (London: Allen and Unwin, 1975).
[121] The spirit of the Snake presumably lived on after its death and became the Devil (cf. Rev. 20:2).

Pelagians and Arminians answer question (1) in the affirmative, Calvinists in the negative.[122] Pelagians answer question (2) in the affirmative, Arminians in the negative.[123]

I begin with general considerations. Our study so far has shown that, whichever way we answer question (1), God is still sovereign. If he wants people to be free to accept or reject the gospel, he can still control the world. The alternative – that people are not free, and can only accept the gospel if God makes them do so – does not make him more sovereign. It only makes his sovereign purpose different. In the first case, he chooses to have as his people those who freely accept his Son. In the second, he chooses individuals on other grounds, and makes them his people.

God need not be confined to one way of working. He could, for example, make voluntary acceptance of the gospel the norm, but save some individuals irresistibly to use them for particular purposes. This would allow a distinction to be drawn between the conversion of, for example, Saul, who could speak of 'One who set me apart from my mother's womb and called [me]' (Acts 9:1–19, Gal. 1:15–16), and those who were 'persuaded' by his preaching (Acts 17:1–4, 28:23–24). We saw in Chapter 4 that a shepherd, when conducting sheep to a new pasture, deals differently with the leading animals, occasionally redirecting their path.

Freedom to accept or reject the gospel does not mean that people can take any credit for accepting it. To be saved, they have to confess their sins, repent of them, and rely utterly on Jesus for forgiveness of them. There is no place for pride of any sort. Jesus told his disciples,

---

[122] Calvinists argue that human beings are totally incapable of even wanting to accept the gospel (the doctrine of 'total depravity'). Rather God chooses whom to save without reference to their responsiveness ('unconditional election'), and so works in them as to bring them to repentance and faith in Christ ('irresistible grace'), and to keep them in this faith ('perseverance of the saints'). Jesus' death was accordingly for them alone ('limited atonement'). See, e.g., Steele *et al.*, *The Five Points of Calvinism*.

[123] Olson, *Arminian Theology*, 17–9.

'Blessed are the poor in spirit, for *theirs* is the kingdom of heaven' (Mat. 5:3).

Freedom also does not mean that evangelists can tell people, 'You are free to accept or reject Jesus.' Their task is to preach the apostolic message, 'God *commands* all people everywhere to repent' (Acts 17:30–31). People may be free to accept or reject, but God puts them under obligation to obey.

In respect to question (2), there is no doubt that God helps people to accept the gospel. He does so in the first place by means of the gospel itself. Jesus commended himself as one to be trusted and followed by his life and teaching. Shortly before his death, he told a crowd, 'I, if I am lifted up from the earth, will draw all peoples to myself' (John 12:32). God has provided a major inducement to faith in the person of Jesus himself.

In addition, Jesus told his disciples that, after his death and resurrection, the Holy Spirit would 'convict the world of sin, of righteousness, and of judgment' (John 16:7–11).

Our conclusion then is that people *can* be free to accept the gospel. That they *are* free is suggested by many passages in the New Testament. A poignant example is Jesus' lament, 'Jerusalem, Jerusalem, … how often I wanted to gather your children together, as a hen gathers her chicks under her wings, and you did not want [it]!' (Mat. 23:37). Another example is the vinedresser's plea in the parable of the Barren Fig Tree, 'Sir, leave it this year also, until I dig round it, and spread manure, and if it bears fruit, [good]; but if not, you can cut it down' (Luke 13:6–9).

However, there are some passages in the New Testament that seem, on first sight, to contradict this. On closer examination, however, they do not, as the following examples show.[124]

---

[124] For a full discussion, see my book, *God's Control over the Universe*, 57–67. To the examples on page 61, add 2 Pet.1:1 [G], 10 [P].

Jesus' teaching

On one occasion, Jesus told his Jewish critics, 'No one can come to me unless the Father who sent me draws him' (John 6:44).[125] The question is, does the Father do this coercively? The answer comes in the next verse, where Jesus explains: 'It is written in the Prophets, "And they shall all be taught by God." Everyone who has heard from the Father and has learned comes to me' (v. 45). This describes a *non-coercive* process: God teaches 'all' ('they shall all be taught by God'), some 'learn' and 'come' ('everyone who has learned comes to me'), others do not. God taught the Jews through 'the Law and the Prophets' (Luke 16:31).

On another occasion, Jesus told Jews who did not come to him, 'You search the Scriptures, because in them you think you have eternal life; and these are they which testify of me; yet you do not want to come to me that you may have life' (John 5:39–40). John later explained that these are the people of whom Isaiah spoke: '[God] has blinded their eyes and hardened their heart' (12:37–41, quoting Isa. 6:9–10). Jesus' statement, 'you do not want to come to me', indicates that the process described by Isaiah was again non-coercive: God 'blinded' and 'hardened' those from coming to Jesus who did not 'want' to come to him.

God's teaching in the Law and the Prophets thus had a *double action* on Jews:[126] it drew those who learnt from it to Jesus, and it hardened those who were unwilling to learn from it. God's acts in Egypt had a similar effect: they hardened Pharaoh (Exod. 7:8 – 14:31), but softened Rahab (Josh. 2:8–11). The Holy Spirit's activity in Acts, 'convicting the world of sin, righteousness, and judgment' (John 16:7–11), was likewise double-acting: it led some to repent (Acts 2:37 etc.), and others to greater hostility (5:33 etc.).

---

[125] Cf. 6:37, 39, 65; 10:29; 17:2, 6, 9, 24; 18:9.

[126] An example of double-action is the effect on smokers of a notice in a hospital waiting room saying, 'Priority will be given to non-smokers'. This will prompt some to give up smoking, but make others angry.

Jesus thanked his Father for drawing to him the kind of people that he did: 'I thank you, Father, Lord of heaven and earth, because you have hidden these things from the learned and clever, and have revealed them to babes' (Mat. 11:25). He went on to say, 'All things have been delivered to me by my Father, and no one knows the Son except the Father, nor does anyone know the Father except the Son, and those to whom the Son wills to reveal him' (v. 27). Jesus here implies that he has the authority to choose those to whom he will reveal his Father. He then exercises his choice: he invites those who are struggling under the burdens imposed by the Pharisees (Mat. 23:1–4), 'Come to me, all you who labour and are burdened, and I will give you rest. Take my yoke upon you and learn from me …' (vv. 28–30).

Jesus calls those who respond 'chosen' (Mat. 24:22 etc.). But the process is again non-coercive: Jesus invites, respondents take his yoke upon them.

Paul's teaching

Romans 8:28–30

In this passage, Paul states that 'we know that [God] works all things together for good for those who love God, for those who are called according to his purpose: that[127] whom he foreknew, he also predestined to be conformed to the image of his Son, so that he might be the first-born among many siblings; and whom he predestined, these he also called; and whom he called, these he also deemed righteous; and whom he deemed righteous, these he also glorified.'

The key to understanding this passage is that 'glorified' is in a past tense.[128] Paul is writing about people who have already died and been glorified. These are the people the writer to the Hebrews describes as 'righteous persons made perfect' (Heb. 12:23) – those in the Old Testament who, 'having obtained a good testimony through faith, did not receive the promise, God having planned something better for us,

---

[127] Gk. *hoti*, as in v. 28.
[128] See my commentary, *Making Sense of Romans* (Seaford: Thankful Books, 2009).

that without us they should not be made perfect' (Heb. 11:39–40). These can be described as 'foreknown by God' (i.e. known before Christ came),[129] 'predestined to be conformed to the image of his Son', 'called according to his purpose', and (through faith) 'deemed righteous'. Then when Christ died and rose again, they were 'perfected' and 'glorified' (cf. John 5:25–29).

Romans 9:6–29

In this passage, Paul begins to deal with a contentious implication of the gospel: that Jews who do not believe in Jesus Christ are lost, even though the Jews are God's chosen people. He argues that God's rejection of Jews does not mean that his promises to the Jews have failed, because God had previously been selective in Jewish history, choosing only one son of Abraham and one son of Isaac (vv. 6–13). Paul further argues that God is not being unrighteous when he chooses in this way because he is acting out of mercy (vv. 14–16). He can have mercy on whom he wants and harden whom he wants (vv. 17–18).[130] In answer to the question, 'Why does he still find fault?', Paul replies, 'Will what is moulded say to the one who moulded it, "Why have you make me like this?" Or has not the potter authority over the clay to make from the same lump one vessel for honour and another for dishonour?' (vv. 19–21). He then comes to the point he has been leading up to: 'What if God, wanting to demonstrate his wrath and to make known his ability, bore with much longsuffering vessels of wrath fit for destruction, and [did this] in order that he might make known the riches of his glory on vessels of mercy, which he prepared for glory, whom also he called – us, not only from the Jews, but also from the Gentiles?' (vv. 22–24). He then cites scriptures to support the inclusion of Gentiles in the second group and of Jews in the first (vv. 25–29).

---

[129] In Jewish thought, 'knowing' a person implied having a relationship with that person (see, e.g., Amos 3:2, Mat. 7:21–23, Gal. 4:8–9).

[130] Paul here emphasizes God's side in the hardening of Pharaoh, as his Jewish opponents would. He is arguing on their ground.

We can understand verses 22–24 as follows.[131] When Paul states that 'God bore with much long-suffering vessels of wrath in order that he might make known the riches of his glory on vessels of mercy', he means that God wanted to make known to the former his blessings on the latter. The purpose of this was to provoke them to jealousy (11:11–14) and lead them to repentance (2:4). The two groups, 'vessels of wrath' and 'vessels of mercy' are not therefore rigid, as Paul makes clear in 11:22–23.

God does not therefore *force* people to be 'vessels of wrath' or 'vessels of mercy'. So why does Paul describe God acting coercively in the previous verses? The answer is to establish God's *right* to act as described in verses 22–24. Paul's argument is that if, as the Jews' own scriptures teach, God has the right to act like a potter, blessing Isaac and Jacob and hardening Pharaoh (vv. 7–21), then he certainly has the right to act as he does through the gospel, dividing Jews and saving Gentiles (vv. 6, 22–29).

1 Corinthians 2:14

Paul writes that 'a natural person does not receive the things of the Spirit of God, for they are folly to him, and he cannot know them, because they are spiritually discerned'. Here, however, 'the things of the Spirit of God' do not refer to the gospel, but to God's 'hidden' wisdom (vv. 7–9) revealed to 'the mature' (v. 6) through the Spirit (vv. 10–16), a wisdom too deep even for some Christians (3:1–3).

2 Corinthians 4:4–6

The apostle says that 'the god of this age has blinded the minds of the unbelieving so that they should not see the light of the gospel of the glory of Christ' (v. 4), while 'God ... has shone in our hearts to [give] the light of the knowledge of the glory of God in the face of [Jesus] Christ' (v. 6). But Paul has just spoken of how he and his co-workers so conducted their ministry as to commend themselves 'to every person's conscience in the sight of God' (vv. 1–2). This implies

---

[131] See *Making Sense of Romans*.

that there is something left in people to appeal to, despite the actions of 'the God of this age'.

Ephesians 1:3−14

Here Paul states that God 'blessed us with every spiritual blessing in the heavenlies in Christ, according as he chose us in him before the foundation of the world, ... having predestined us to adoption through Jesus Christ to himself ...; in whom also we were allotted, having been predestined according to the purpose of him who works all things according to what he decides he wants ...' (vv. 3−5, 11).

The meaning of this passage turns on the meaning of 'chose us in him before the foundation of the world'. This could mean that God chose us 'to be united with Christ' or 'through being united with Christ'. In the latter case, God chose *Christ* 'before the foundation of the world' (cf. Luke 9:35 $P^{45, 75}$, John 17:24, 1 Pet. 1:20, etc.), and we partake of his chosenness through being united with him. The second interpretation is favoured by 2:6 ('[God] raised [us] with [Christ] and seated [us] with [him] in the heavenlies in Christ Jesus'). We do not sit in the heavenlies in ourselves: we sit in them by being united with Jesus who sits in them.

Ephesians 2:1−10

Paul goes on to tell his readers that they, along with other believers, were 'dead in trespasses and sins' until 'God made us alive with Christ' (vv. 1−5). In its context, this means that God made *Christ* alive, and makes us alive with him (vv. 5−7) 'through faith' (vv. 8−9).

In English translations of verse 8, Paul seems to say that faith is a gift of God, but in the Greek it is salvation that is a gift (*pistis* is feminine, *touto* is neuter).

In verse 10, Paul says, 'we are [God's] handiwork, created in Christ Jesus for good works, which God laid down beforehand, so that we might walk in them'. This could mean that God has a particular plan for each believer, but it is more likely to mean that he has a general plan for all believers – that they should do the good works Paul exhorts the Ephesians to do in Chapters 4–6.

Philippians 2:12–13

Paul told the Philippians, 'work out your own salvation with fear and trembling; for it is God who works in you both to want and to work for his good pleasure.' Here Paul speaks of God working in believers even to 'want' his good pleasure, but not so coercively as to take away their responsibility to 'work out' their salvation. Paul's point is that believers should work out their salvation '*with fear and trembling*' because it is '*God*' who is working in them.

Other teaching

James 2:14–26

These verses could be taken to mean that believers can achieve salvation entirely by their own efforts ('by works'). James is, however, countering antinomianism, the idea that people can be saved irrespective of how they live. His argument is that good works must accompany faith, not that they can secure salvation (cf. Eph. 2:8–10).[132]

1 Peter 1:1–2

Peter describes his readers as 'chosen exiles of [the] dispersion of Pontus, Galatia, Cappadocia, Asia, and Bithynia, according to [the] foreknowledge of God [the] Father, in sanctification of [the] Spirit, unto obedience, and sprinkling of [the] blood of Jesus Christ'.

The key to understanding this passage is that Peter's readers were Jewish – he refers to them as 'exiles of the dispersion'. God could therefore have 'known' them (been in relationship with them[133]) before they heard the gospel (cf. Rom. 8:29, 11:2). Peter says that God, 'according to' his relationship with them, chose them to be Christians.

---

[132] See my *Biblical Light on Contemporary Issues*, Chap. 3.
[133] See note under 'Romans 8:28–30'.

The implication is that they were in a state to accept the gospel when they heard it (John 3:21; cf. Cornelius, Acts 10).[134]

Apostasy

'Can Christians commit apostasy?' This is another thorny question. Calvinists say 'No',[135] Pelagians 'Yes'; Arminians are divided.[136]

On this, the New Testament itself seems divided. Some scriptures seem to say that Christians can never be cut off from God; others seem to warn that they can be.

This difference arises because the authors are addressing different problems. In the first case, the issue is whether Jesus can keep followers safe in any tribulation they pass through. The answer is that he can (John 10:27–30, Rom. 8:31–39). In the second case, the issue is what happens if people (1) profess to follow Jesus but continue a life of sin, or (2) start to follow him and then not merely falter but completely fall away. The answer is that they will be rejected [(1) Mat. 7:21–23; (2) John 15:1–6, Rom. 11:22, Heb. 6:4–6, 2 Pet. 2:20–22].[137]

What the authors say therefore coheres. In effect, God will not cut off those who fear being cut off, but will cut off those who do not (cf. Deut. 29:18–20).

---

[134] See further under 'Those who never hear'.
[135] The doctrine of the 'perseverance of the saints'.
[136] Olson, *Arminian Theology*, 32. For opposing views, see R.T. Kendall, *Once Saved, Always Saved* (Belfast: Ambassador, 1983; Carlisle: Paternoster, 1997); David Pawson, *Once Saved, Always Saved?* (London: Hodder and Stoughton, 1996).
[137] Paul's reference in 1 Corinthians 3:11–15 to a man being saved in spite of his work ('as through fire') must be understood in its context. He is referring to *teachers* (vv. 1–10) whose teaching does not promote lasting Christian qualities (cf. 13:8–13). He does not say the same of teachers whose teaching is destructive (vv. 16–17).

Those who never hear

Theologians differ over the question of what happens to those who never hear the gospel.[138] Jesus told his disciples, 'I am the way, and the truth, and the life. No one comes to the Father except through me' (John 14:6). Peter said, 'there is salvation in no one else, for there is no other name under heaven given among humankind by which we must be saved' (Acts 4:12). Does this mean that all those who never hear of Jesus are lost?

The Bible does not address this question directly. However, it does give some clues, from which tentative conclusions can be drawn.[139]

The first clue comes in the book of Jonah. God told Jonah to go to the evil, pagan city of Nineveh and preach against it (1:1–2). After Jonah's dramatic disobedience and deliverance (1:3 – 2:10), God told him a second time to go to the city and preach his message to it (3:1–2). This time Jonah went and told the people, 'Yet forty days, and Nineveh shall be overthrown' (vv. 3–4). This led them to repent (vv. 5–9), as a result of which God did not do to them what he said he would do (v. 10). This upset Jonah (4:1–4), leading God to afflict him with the loss of something that was valuable to him (vv. 5–8). Reminding him of how he felt about this, God said to him, 'And should I not pity Nineveh, that great city, in which there are more than a hundred and twenty thousand people who do not know their right hand from their left …?' (vv. 9–11). The lesson is that God is concerned for people who know little about him.

A second clue comes in Paul's letter to the Romans. Here he explains how God can judge those who do not have his law by how they act in relation to such law as they have: 'For whenever Gentiles, who do not have [the] law, by nature do the things of the law, these, not having [the] law, to themselves are [the] law: who demonstrate

---

[138] See, e.g., John Sanders, *No Other Name* (Grand Rapids: Eerdmans, 1992).
[139] I have not included 1 Timothy 4:10 because of uncertainty over the meaning of *malista* [see T.C. Skeat, *JTS* 30 (1979), 173–7].

[that] the work of the law [is] written in their hearts, their conscience bearing witness with [this], and their reckonings between one another accusing or even excusing [them], in the day in which, according to my gospel, God judges the secrets of humankind through Christ Jesus' (2:14–16).[140]

A third clue is provided by the men and women of faith under the old covenant mentioned earlier.[141] The writer to the Hebrews says that these, 'having been commended through their faith, did not receive the promise, God having provided something better for us, in order that, without us, they should not be made perfect' (11:39–40). He goes on to tell his readers that they have come, not to Mount Sinai, but 'to Mount Zion, and to the city of the living God, the heavenly Jerusalem, and to myriads of angels in full assembly, and to the congregation of the first-born who are enrolled in heaven, and to God, the judge of all, and to the spirits of righteous ones made perfect, and to Jesus, the mediator of a new covenant, and to the sprinkled blood that speaks better than [that of] Abel' (12:18–24). Here 'the spirits of righteous ones made perfect' are evidently the spirits of those of whom the writer earlier wrote, 'without us, they should not be made perfect'. They are, in other words, men and women of faith under the old covenant now made perfect through Jesus.[142] This example shows how God can accept people who do not know Jesus, and subsequently perfect them through him.

A second example of this is God's acceptance of the Roman army officer, Cornelius (Acts 10:1). Luke says that he was 'devout and feared God with all his household, gave alms generously to the people, and prayed to God always' (v. 2). An angel told him, 'Your prayers

---

[140] Paul is not speaking here about Christians. He does not say that the Gentiles concerned have the law itself 'written in their hearts', as Jeremiah prophesied that Christians would have (Jer. 31:31–34). He only says that they have 'the work of the law' written in their hearts (*grapton* agrees with *ergon* not *nomou*). This presumably refers to what the law requires.
[141] Under the discussion of Romans 8:28–30 and 1 Peter 1:1–2.
[142] Paul speaks of God 'passing over' sins until Jesus' propitiatory death (Rom. 3:21–26).

and your alms have gone up for a memorial before God' (vv. 3–4). The angel then told him to send for Peter (vv. 5–8), and God revealed to Peter that he should not refuse to help a Gentile (vv. 9–22). Peter accordingly went to Cornelius (vv. 23–33), saying, 'Truly I grasp that God is not partial, but in every nation anyone who fears him and works righteousness is acceptable to him' (vv. 34–35). He then proceeded to tell Cornelius about Jesus (vv. 36–43). Cornelius so embraced what he heard that God gave him the Holy Spirit while Peter was still speaking (vv. 44–48). When Peter told the other apostles about this (11:1–17), they concluded, 'Then God has also granted to Gentiles the repentance that leads to life' (v. 18).

These clues suggest that God can save those who never hear the gospel by judging them according to the light that they have, and then perfecting them through Jesus. Thus, he can judge their response to what they can know of him through 'the things that have been made' (Rom. 1:19–20), their endeavour to do what they believe to be right (Rom. 2:14–16), and their remorse when they fail to do this (Psa. 51:17). He can then perfect those he accepts, after they die, through Jesus, as he did the Old Testament saints (Heb. 12:23).

This does not mean that Christians need not spread the gospel, because God wants people to live in the light, not in ignorance. While he accepted Cornelius, he still wanted him to hear about Jesus. As Paul told Timothy, 'God … wants *all* people to be saved and to come to a *full* knowledge (*epignōsis*) of the truth' (1 Tim. 2:1–4).

Jesus accordingly told his disciples, 'You are the light of the world …' (Mat. 5:14–16), and, after his resurrection, gave them the Great Commission: 'Go and make disciples of all the nations, baptizing them into the name of the Father, and of the Son, and of the Holy Spirit, [and] teaching them to observe all that I have commanded you' (Mat. 28:19–20). Here 'disciple' (*mathētēs*) literally means 'learner'.

Conclusion

We have seen that God can allow human beings to have free will while controlling everything that happens in the world. This means that we can do equal justice to passages in the Bible that speak of God's sovereignty and to those that imply human freedom. These can be held together in a fully consistent way.

CHAPTER 6
Prayer

Prayer is problematic. Sometimes we pray for something, and what we pray for happens. Often what we pray for does not happen. Occasionally, what we pray for does not happen for us, but does happen for someone else who prays a similar prayer. How do we make sense of these experiences?

In some cases, the problem lies with us. James told his readers, 'You ask and do not receive, because you ask wrongly, to spend it on your pleasures' (Jas. 4:3). Peter told husbands to honour their wives, lest their prayers be hindered (1 Pet. 3:7). However, even when we pray unselfishly, and honour others, we can experience the difficulties I have described.

In these cases, a simple answer is to say that we often do not pray according to God's will. His ways are not our ways, and his thoughts are not our thoughts (Isa. 55:8–9). When what we ask for does not happen, it is because God wants something better to happen. He still hears our prayers but answers them in a different way (cf. Rom. 8:26–27).

However, this does not help us when we cannot see something better happening, and when we feel that God is not answering *any* of our prayers. When we feel like this, we can start to doubt whether we are a Christian, or whether God answers prayer at all.

Here I present a fuller answer to the problem.

God's ability to answer prayer

As the creator of the universe, God has all the power he needs to answer prayer. Jesus prefaced his prayer in the Garden of Gethsemane, 'Father, all things are possible for you' (Mark 14:36).

God can grant requests in essentially three ways.[143] If someone asks for X, and the natural flow of events is leading to X, he can simply let this flow take place. If, however, the natural flow is leading to Y, he can intervene at the point Y would happen and bring about X in an openly miraculous way. Alternatively, he can intervene in the natural flow of events at a point before Y would happen and make the flow lead to X instead. An example of this is when Paul was caught in a storm in the Mediterranean Sea (Acts 27). In response to his prayer, God made the boat run aground on the tiny island of Malta. He did not do this directly – the storm still raged; the boat still drifted and tossed. No one saw him doing anything. Yet he so controlled the storm that Paul was kept safe.

Factors affecting how God answers prayer

Human freedom

I here assume that God has given human beings freedom. I explained in Chapters 4 and 5 how this does not prevent him from controlling the world and working out his purposes in it. I further assume that God wants human beings to worship him, trust him, and obey him (Deut. 6:4–5 etc.).

Now for men and women to be able to do this effectively, God must reveal himself to them so that they know what to do; but for them to be able to do this voluntarily, he must also hide himself from them so that they are not forced to do it. He has therefore carefully to measure his activity in the world, so as to make faith possible, but not pre-empt it (cf. Deut. 29:29; Isa. 45:15; Mat. 12: 38–40, 13:10–17; John 20:24–29; etc.).

---

[143] See Chapters 4 and 5.

What this means for prayer is that God rarely answers petitions directly, in an obviously miraculous way. If he answered them in this way very often, human beings would be bound to believe, which is not his intention. His intention is that they should 'walk by faith, not by sight' (2 Cor. 5:7). He accordingly more often answers petitions indirectly, in ways that can less readily be interpreted as answers to prayer other than 'by faith'.

God's respect for human freedom also means that he does not continually give people the things they ask for even indirectly. He gives them enough of what they ask for to encourage faith, but not so much as to make faith easy. [Jesus did say, 'whatever you ask in my name, this I will do' (John 14:13–14 etc.), but this is a conditional promise, as I discuss later.]

Freedom of others

God's respect for human freedom also constrains his response to prayers for others. We may wish to ask him to make someone do something good, or to stop someone from doing something bad, but we cannot expect him ordinarily to do this. We can only ask him to *encourage* someone to do something good, or to *discourage* someone from doing something bad, or to *compensate* for someone's action. We cannot expect him to override a person's freedom other than very exceptionally.

So, for example, we may want someone we know to be saved. But we know from Jesus' parable of the Barren Fig Tree that God does not force people to repent, but rather gives them time and suitable conditions in which to do so (Luke 13:6–9). So we cannot pray, 'O God, *make* John repent,' and expect God to do this, but we can pray, 'O God, encourage John to repent.'

However, we do not have to recast all our prayers in this way, as long as we understand how God will answer them. Thus, Jesus taught us to pray, 'your will be done, on earth as it is in heaven' (Mat. 6:10), knowing that God will not force human beings to be obedient (cf. Mat. 23:37 etc.). He likewise prayed himself that believers 'may all be one'

(John 17) knowing that, on earth, they would not be. So we can pray, 'O God, save John,' as long as we understand how God will answer this. Indeed Paul encouraged prayers for the salvation of others (1 Tim. 2:1–4).

The Curse

A further constraint on prayer is imposed by the events described in Genesis 3.[144] Because of the fall of Adam and Eve, God cursed the natural order, introducing into it pain, toil, and death. As a result, 'the whole creation' now 'groans and travails' (Rom. 8:18–22). Even believers 'groan within themselves' (v. 23). One day the Curse will be removed, but this still lies in the future, when there will be 'a new heaven and a new earth' (Rev. 21:1–5) and 'no more curse' (Rev. 22:1–5).

Thus, believers cannot expect God to remove the effects of the Curse in this life, other than very exceptionally. Jesus did remove effects of the Curse when he was on earth (he healed the sick, restored the disabled, and even raised the dead), but he emphasized the temporariness of this. When he came across a blind man, he told his disciples, 'We must work the works of him who sent me while it is day; night is coming when no one can work. *While I am in the world*, I am the light of the world' (John 9:4–5). It is true that he later told his disciples that they would do 'greater' works than he did (John 14:12), but 'greater' here must refer to spread of the gospel: their works could not have been greater in any other way. Rather, he went on to warn them, 'In the world you will have tribulation' (John 16:33). This included, besides persecution, effects of the Curse: famine (Acts 11:27–30), poverty (Gal. 2:10), sickness (Gal. 4:13–14, Phil. 2:25–27, 1 Tim. 5:23, 2 Tim. 4:20), natural disasters (2 Cor.11:23–28), and death (1 Cor. 15:6).

---

[144] See Chapter 3.

Thus, Christians can only pray for removal of effects of the Curse in the way Jesus prayed in the Garden of Gethsemane:[145]

> 'Father, all things are possible for you. Remove this cup from me. But not what I want, but what you want.' (Mark 14:36)

The Devil

Another effect of the events in Genesis 3 is that the Snake became the Devil.[146] God punished him by reducing his powers, but did not completely remove them (Gen. 3:14–15). Only in the last days will God render the Devil impotent (Rev. 20:10).

What this means is that the Devil also plays a part in what happens in the world. Christians can pray that God will deliver them from evil (Mat. 6:13), but not that he will take it completely away (Mat. 13:24–30, 36–43).

Refinement of faith

A further constraint on prayer is God's desire to *refine* the faith of his people. This involves putting them into situations [or allowing the Devil to put them into situations (Job 1–2)[147]] in which maintaining faith is difficult, and holding on to it leads to a deepening of it.

The apostles taught believers to expect God to refine their faith in this way (Rom. 5:1–5, 8:17–39; 2 Cor. 1:3–7; Heb. 12:4–11; Jas. 1:2–4; 1 Pet. 1:6–7, 4:12–19). Paul even made the anguished cry, 'Abba, Father!', proof of having the Spirit (Rom. 8:15–17).

All this means that God treats believers in two very different ways. On the one hand, he encourages young believers by answering their prayers in ways that they can see. On the other hand, he tests the faith of older believers by *not* answering their prayers in ways that they can

---

[145] On James 5:13–18, see my *Biblical Light on Contemporary Issues* (Hayesville: AJBT, 2018), Chap. 13.

[146] See Chapters 3–5.

[147] See Chapter 7.

see. Paul prayed three times for his 'thorn in the flesh' to be removed, but the Lord said to him, 'My grace is sufficient for you, for my power is made perfect in weakness' (2 Cor. 12:7–10).

God also treats unbelievers in two opposing ways. On the one hand, he encourages all but the most hardened unbelievers to repent by making life unpleasant for them when they sin. On the other hand, he leaves the most hardened unbelievers to their own devices (cf. Rom. 1:18–32) and lets them (for so long) prosper. This explains the anguished cry of the psalmist over the prosperity of the wicked (Psa. 73).

God thus allows some people to prosper and others to suffer, as summarized in the following table. For those whose belief or unbelief is weak, he acts in one way; for those for whom it is strong, he acts in another. The result is an inversion of experience as faith or wickedness grows.

	Believers	Unbelievers
Weak	prosper	suffer
Strong	suffer	prosper

Jesus' teaching

Jesus taught his disciples to pray in faith (Mark 11:22–24). He further told them, as I mentioned earlier, 'whatever you ask in my name, this I will do' (John 14:13–14; 15:7, 16; 16:23–24). However, praying 'in the name of' Jesus implies praying in a way that is consistent with his teaching. This is explicit in John 15:7: 'If you remain in me *and my words remain in you*, ask whatever you want, and it shall be given to you.'

Christians can therefore pray for the things Jesus taught – for God's name to be revered, his rule to come, and his will to be done; for daily bread, forgiveness of sins, and protection from evil (Mat. 6:9–13). Here 'daily bread' doubtless includes the 'bread of life' (John 6) and the Holy Spirit (Luke 11:1–13), given to enable believers to live as they should

(Rom. 6:15 – 8:14, Gal. 5:13–26, 2 Pet. 1:3–11). Christian leaders can also ask Jesus to help them to resolve conflicts in church (Mat. 18:15–20).

Jesus' teaching therefore leads us to expect answers to prayer, but only in certain areas. Many of the things we ask for lie outside these areas. In other areas, we have to say, 'not what I want, but what you want' (Mark 14:36), and rely on the Spirit to pray correctly for us (Rom. 8:26–27).

Conclusion

God's ways are not our ways, and his thoughts are not our thoughts (Isa. 55:8–9). Yet Scripture does throw some light on why God apparently answers some prayers and not others. He works in the world to bring people to faith and then to refine their faith. This leads him to treat them in contrary ways. We may sometimes feel that he is not answering our prayers, but, in reality, he is working in all things for our good (Rom. 8:28–30).

CHAPTER 7

What the Book of Job Teaches about Suffering

Job is an important book in the Bible. It is one of the longest (42 chapters), and deals with an important subject, namely suffering. It is, however, difficult. This is partly because of its length, which makes it difficult for the reader to keep track of where it is going. It is also because much of it is in poetry, the precise meaning of which is sometimes obscure.[148] Preachers accordingly rarely speak on it, except for Job's statement made famous by Handel's aria, 'I know that my Redeemer liveth'.

Because of these difficulties, Daniel Estes says that, to study the book properly, one needs to acquire a good understanding of poetic Hebrew, and to go through the book line by line in detail.[149] This is something few ministers have time to do, let alone lay members of congregations.

An alternative approach, I suggest, is to read the book through quickly, passing over puzzling passages, and not stopping until reaching the end. In this way, the reader can see where the narrative is leading, and the lessons it is intended to teach. He or she can then go back and study key passages in more detail, using commentaries on the Hebrew text.[150]

---

[148] For example, 19:26 literally reads: 'And after my skin (masc.), they flay this (fem.), yet from my flesh, I shall/would (imperf.) see God.'

[149] Daniel J. Estes, 'Communicating the book of Job in the twenty-first century,' *Themelios* 40 (2015), 243–52.

[150] E.g., Samuel Rolles Driver and George Buchanan Gray, *A Critical and Exegetical Commentary on the Book of Job* (Edinburgh: T. & T. Clark, 1921); David J.A. Clines, *Job 1–20*, Word Biblical Commentary [WBC] Vol. 17 (Dallas, Texas: Word Books, 1989), *Job 21–37*, WBC Vol. 18A (Nashville,

Here I give a short exposition of the book arrived at in this way. The exposition is sufficiently short to enable ministers to base a single sermon on it. Preaching series of sermons on Job is difficult because the lessons it teaches only come out at the end.

Exposition

Who Job was (1:1–5)

The book of Job introduces us to him. It describes him as a righteous man whom God had greatly prospered:

> ¹There was a man in the land of Uz [east of the Jordon] whose name was Job. That man was blameless and upright, fearing God and turning away from evil. ²There were born to him seven sons and three daughters. ³His possessions were seven thousand sheep, three thousand camels, five thousand yoke of oxen, five hundred female donkeys, and very many servants, so that that man was greater than all the sons of the east.

What happened to him (1:6–2:10)

The book of Job goes on to describe how Satan challenged God about Job and was allowed to put him to the test:

> ⁶Now came a day when the sons of God [angels?] came to present themselves before the LORD, and Satan also came among them. ⁷The LORD said to Satan, 'From where have you come?' Satan answered the LORD and said, 'From roving on the earth, and from walking back and forth on it.' ⁸And the LORD said to Satan, 'Have you directed your attention to my servant Job? For there is no one like him on the earth, a man blameless and upright, fearing God and turning away from evil.' ⁹Then Satan answered the LORD and said, 'Does Job fear God for nothing? ¹⁰Have

---

Tennessee: Nelson, 2006), *Job 38–42*, WBC Vol. 18B (Nelson, 2011) (all republished by Zondervan, Nashville, 2015).

you not put a hedge around him, and his house, and all his estate? You have blessed the work of his hands, and his possessions have increased in the land. ¹¹But surely, put out your hand now and touch all that is his [and see] if he will not curse* you to your face.' ¹²And the LORD said to Satan, 'Behold, all that is his is in your hand. Only on him do not put out your hand.' So Satan went out from the presence of the LORD.

*Heb. *bārak*, 'bless', here used in a bad sense.

Satan then proceeded to take everything away from Job (1:13–19). Job, however, responded to this well:

²⁰Then Job rose up, tore his robe, shaved his head, and fell down on the ground and worshipped. ²¹He said, 'Naked I came out of the womb of my mother, and naked I shall return there [the 'womb' of the grave]. The LORD gave, and the LORD has taken away; blessed be the name of the LORD.' ²²In all this, Job did not sin, nor charge God with wrong.

This scenario is then repeated (2:1–8). Satan says to God that Job is responding well because he still has his health: 'Take this away and he will curse you to your face.' So God allows Satan to afflict Job with painful sores from his head to his feet.

Again Job responds well, at least to start with (2:9–10).

Job's friends (2:11–13)

The book of Job now introduces us to his friends:

¹¹Now three friends of Job heard of all this evil that had come upon him, and they came each one from his own place: Eliphaz the Temanite, Bildad the Shuhite, and Zophar the Naamathite. They met together to come to console him and to comfort him. ¹²When they lifted up their eyes from afar and did not recognize him, they lifted up

their voice and wept. Each one tore his robe, and they sprinkled dust on their heads towards the heavens. ¹³And they sat down with him on the ground seven days and seven nights. No one spoke to him a word, for they saw that his suffering was very great.

Job expresses his anguish (3)[151]

Job finally speaks. In vivid language, he says that he wishes that he had not been born (vv. 1–10). He goes on to question why God kept him alive at birth (vv. 11–19) and why he allows people to live when they want to die (vv. 20–23). He concludes:[152]

> ²³[Why is life given] to a man whose way is hidden,
>   whom God has hemmed in?
> ²⁴For my sighing comes before my food,
>   and my groanings are poured out like waters.
> ²⁵For the dreadful thing I dreaded has come upon me,
>   and what I feared has come to me.
> ²⁶I am not at ease, I am not quiet;
>   I am not at rest, yet turmoil comes.

Job's friends argue with him (4–31)

Job's questioning prompts his friends to speak. They took the simple view that his suffering must be due to some sin he has committed, and that what he should do is repent.

Job, however, disagreed. He was not aware of any sin that would account for his suffering. He told his friends this, and that the line they were taking did not help him.

But his friends stuck to their view, and this led to a long argument between them. This argument forms a major part of the book, its length serving to heighten the drama.

---

[151] Single figures refer to chapters.
[152] Following on v. 20.

The course of the argument is as follows.[153]

- ***Eliphaz speaks.*** He tells Job that it is the righteous who prosper and the wicked who do not (4) and counsels him to accept God's correction (5).

- ○ ***Job replies.*** He says that Eliphaz's words do not help him (6) and continues to express his anguish (7).

- ***Bildad speaks.*** He tells Job to plead to God for mercy (8).

- ○ ***Job replies.*** He says that, what he would like to do, argue with God, he cannot, God being who he is (9). He goes on to complain to God about his suffering (10).

- ***Zophar speaks.*** He tells Job that he should not speak like this. He should repent; God would then bless him (11).

- ○ ***Job replies.*** He says that God acts as he wills (12), and that his friends speak wrongly (13). He goes on to ask God to listen to him (14).

- ***Eliphaz speaks again.*** He accuses Job of speaking emptily: it is the wicked who suffer (15).

- ○ ***Job replies.*** He tells his friends that they do not help (16), and continues to complain about his situation (17). Frustrated that they do not accept what he says, he tells them that he feels sure that there is someone in heaven who will one day vindicate him (16:19–21).

- ***Bildad speaks again.*** He tells Job to be sensible: the people God punishes are the wicked (18).

- ○ ***Job replies.*** He says that his friends have let him down, and that everyone is against him (19). He is again sure,

---

[153] When preaching on Job, I go through this quickly, turning over the relevant pages of my Bible as I do. This gives hearers a feel for the intensity of the argument, and how long it goes on for.

however, that someone will one day vindicate him (v. 25, 'I know that my protector[154] lives').

- **Zophar speaks again.** He says that he must reply: God brings suffering on the wicked (20).

○ **Job replies.** He tells Zophar that he is speaking nonsense: wicked people prosper (21).

- **Eliphaz speaks for a third time.** He tells Job explicitly that he is suffering because of his sins. He should repent; God would then bless him (22).

○ **Job replies.** He says that, if he could find God, he would plead his cause, but cannot find him (23). God will indeed deal with the wicked, but very much in his own time (24).

- **Bildad speaks for a third time.** He says that, with God being all-powerful, humans cannot be righteous (25).

○ **Job replies.** He says that what Bildad has said does not help him. He accepts that God is all-powerful (26). While insisting that his friends' judgment of him is wrong, he further accepts, as they have been saying, that God will deal with the wicked (27), and that wisdom is to be found only in God (28). He goes on to recall happier days, when people respected him and God blessed him (29), and laments that all this has changed: people are now against him and God does not answer (30). He concludes that, if he has broken any commandments, it would be right for God to judge him, but he has not (31).

---

[154] Heb. *gō'ēl*, usually translated 'redeemer'. This has to be understood in its context, following 16:19–21, not in its New Testament sense. Driver and Gray render it 'vindicator', Clines 'champion'. Compare, e.g., Prov. 23:11. Job's belief in a *gō'ēl* does not stop him complaining.

An unexpected interjection (32–37)

At this point, the story of Job takes an unexpected turn. A younger man comes into it:

> ³²:¹So these three men ceased from answering Job, because he was righteous in his own eyes. ²Then the anger of Elihu the son of Barachel the Buzite, of the family of Ram, burned. His anger burned against Job because he had justified himself rather than God. ³His anger also burned against his three friends because they had found no answer, yet had condemned Job. ⁴Elihu had waited to have words with Job because they were older in age than he. ⁵When Elihu saw that there was no answer in the mouths of the three men, his anger burned.

So, he speaks. He says that he has not spoken up to this point out of deference to the older men (32:6–22). He proceeds to tell Job that he is wrong to complain to God about his suffering. He explains that God brings suffering on individuals, not merely to punish them as the older men had implied in much of what they said,[155] but to *correct* them (33). He describes how God may speak to a man 'in a dream, a vision of the night' (vv. 13–18) and chasten him 'with pain on his bed, and continual strife in his bones' (vv. 19–22), but accepts the man's penitence and 'restores his righteousness' (vv. 23–28).[156] He concludes:

> ²⁹Lo, God does all these things
>   two times or three with a man,
> ³⁰to bring back his soul from the pit,
>   [for him] to be lit with the light of the living.

---

[155] Eliphaz briefly mentioned correction at the beginning (5:17), but as the argument proceeded, the line taken by the older men hardened [compare Eliphaz's final contribution (22)].

[156] In verses 23–25, Elihu refers to 'an intermediary' (Heb. *lûṣ*). In the setting of the Old Testament, this is presumably a priest (cf. Heb. 5:1–3). Elihu also refers to 'a ransom' (Heb. *kōper*), presumably an animal for sacrifice (Lev. 4:1–6:7; cf. Job 42:8).

Elihu goes on to emphasize that God is God. He is altogether above us. We human beings are not in a position to question him (34–35). His greatness is seen in the wonders of the created order (36–37). Elihu calls on Job to recognize this:

> $^{37:14}$'Listen to this, O Job;
> > stand still and consider God's wonders.
>
> ^{15}Do you know when God put them in place,
> > and makes the light[ening] of his clouds to shine?
>
> ^{16}Do you know about the balancing of the clouds,
> > the wonderful works of the one perfect in knowledge,
>
> ^{17}you whose garments are hot,
> > when the earth is still from the [gentle] south wind?
>
> ^{18}Can you, with him, spread out the skies,
> > [pictured as] strong as a cast [metal] mirror?'

God speaks to Job (38–41)

At this point, God speaks. What he says follows on from what Elihu has said. Elihu said, 'Look at the wonders of the created order'; God says, 'Look at my handiwork':

> $^{38:1}$Then the LORD answered Job out of the tempest and said:
>
> ^{2}'Who is this that darkens counsel
> > by words without knowledge?
>
> ^{3}Gird up your loins now like a man,
> > for I will question you, and you will enlighten me.
>
> ^{4}Where were you when I laid the earth's foundations?
> > Declare if you know and understand.
>
> ^{5}Who determined its measurements, for [surely] you know!
> > Or who has stretched a line upon it?
>
> ^{6}On what were its bases sunk,
> > or who laid its cornerstone,
>
> ^{7}when the morning stars sang together
> > and all the sons of God shouted for joy?'

God continues to challenge Job in this way, first over the physical universe (38:8–38) and then all the animals (38:39–39:30). This has the effect of silencing Job (40:1–5). God goes on to ask him whether he has the ability to justify himself, seeing that he does not have the ability to capture a big beast[157] (40:6–24), still less tame a big reptile[158] (41).[159]

Job responds (42:1–6)

¹Then Job answered the LORD and said:

²'I know that you can do all things,
   and no purpose is withheld from you.
³[You asked,] "Who is this hiding counsel without knowledge?" [38:2]
   Therefore [yes] I declared but did not understand
   things too wonderful for me, things I did not know.
⁴[You said,] "Listen, now, and I will speak;
   I will question you and you will enlighten me." [38:3]
⁵I had heard of you [yes] by the hearing of the ear,
   but now my eye has seen you.
⁶Therefore I despise myself,
   and repent in dust and ashes.'

God speaks to Job's friends (42:7–9)

God goes on to speak to Job's friends:

⁷And it was that, after the LORD had spoken these words to Job, the LORD said to Eliphaz the Temanite, 'My anger burns against you and your two friends, for you have not spoken about me what is right, as my servant Job has. ⁸Now therefore take for yourselves seven bulls and seven rams and go to my servant Job, and offer up a burnt offering for yourselves. And my servant Job will pray for you. I will surely accept [his presenting to me] his face so as not to deal with you according to your folly, for you have not spoken about me what is right, as my servant Job has.'

---

[157] Heb. *bᵉhēmôṯ* (behemoth), possibly the hippopotamus.
[158] Heb. *liwyāṯān* (leviathan), possibly the crocodile.
[159] Some scholars think that these animals have a mystical significance, but the descriptions are of the animals as animals.

> ⁹So Eliphaz the Temanite, Bildad the Shuhite, and Zophar the Naamathite went and did as the LORD had spoken to them, and the LORD accepted Job's [presenting of his] face.

Here God compares favourably what Job had said with what his friends had said. This does not mean that everything Job had said was right, as he has just acknowledged (vv. 1–6). Notice that God does not condemn the younger man, Elihu.

God restores Job's prosperity (42:10–17)

God then makes Job prosperous again:

> ¹⁰The LORD turned the captivity of Job [released him from his suffering] when he prayed for his friends. The LORD added to Job double of all that had been his. ¹¹Then came to him all his brothers and all his sisters, and all who knew him before, and they ate bread with him in his house. And they sympathized with him and comforted him concerning all the evil that the LORD had brought upon him. Each of them gave to him a piece of money and a ring of gold.
>
> ¹²So the LORD blessed the latter days of Job more than the first. …

This blessing is spelt out in the verses that follow.

Notice that the narrator here attributes Job's sufferings to God. It was Satan who had afflicted them, but it was God who had given him permission to do so.

Lessons

From the above exposition, we can draw the following lessons from the book of Job:[160]

- The main lesson is that a person's suffering is not necessarily due to his or her sins. Job's three friends were wrong to make this link.

---

[160] Compare Eric Ortlund, 'Five truths for sufferers from the book of Job,' *Themelios* 40 (2015), 253–62.

The key verse is 42:7: 'the LORD said to Eliphaz the Temanite, "My anger burns against you and your two friends, *for you have not spoken about me what is right*"'.

So while a person's suffering can be due to his or her sins (1 Cor. 11:27–30), it may not be. God may allow Satan to inflict suffering to demonstrate a person's faith and obedience, and, in the process, refine them.[161] In the New Testament, Jesus is said to have 'learned obedience from what he suffered' (Heb. 5:7–10) and to have been made 'perfect through sufferings' (Heb. 2:10), becoming thereby 'the leader and perfecter of the [exercise of] faith' (Heb. 12:2).[162] Peter wrote of trials 'testing' faith (1 Pet. 1:3–9), and James of this testing 'producing steadfastness (*hupomonē*)', citing Job's testing as an example (Jas. 1:2–4, 5:10–11). Paul wrote in a similar vein: 'tribulation produces steadfastness, and steadfastness proof [of character] (*dokimē*), and proof [of character] hope' (Rom. 5:3–4).

Suffering of this kind is therefore part of God's programme to discipline his people (Prov. 3:11–12, Rev. 3:19–20). Discipline is broader than refinement because it includes correction, but the objective is the same: to develop faith and obedience. Elihu spoke about correction at length (33:14–30). He thus went some way towards explaining Job's suffering, but not all the way. Job's suffering was for refinement, not correction.

Jesus taught that a person's suffering is not necessarily due to his or her sins, but in different contexts from Job's suffering (a man born blind, John 9:1–3a; tragedies in Jerusalem, Luke 13:1–7). In these cases, the suffering was due to the world being as it is, the world being as it is as a result of the Fall (Gen. 3).[163]

- A second lesson of the book of Job is that Job-like suffering does not last for ever. There is an end to it (Jas. 5:11b). This may come

---

[161] Ortlund discounts refinement, but the New Testament references support this.
[162] I take *archēgos* to have the same meaning in the New Testament as in the Septuagint.
[163] See Chapter 3.

in this world, as it did for Job, or in the world to come, as it did for Jesus (Heb. 12:2).

- A third lesson is that those who are reckoned to be wise are not necessarily so. At the time of Job, the elderly were reckoned to be wise (15:10), but in the narrative they are shown up by the younger man. Today, young people tend to think they are wise. All need to remember, as Job himself did (28:28): 'The fear of the LORD is the beginning of wisdom' (Prov. 9:10).

PART III
OTHER ISSUES

CHAPTER 8

Demon-possession

The Bible presupposes the existence of demons. These may be free agents or subject to the Devil. If they are free agents, God can control their actions in a similar way to those of other agents (Chap. 4).

There are, however, difficulties in reconciling what the New Testament says about demon-possession and modern science. According to the New Testament, evil spirits[164] can enter human beings (Luke 11:24–26), and produce fits (Mark 1:26), insanity (Mark 5:1–5), dumbness (Mat. 9:32), blindness and dumbness (Mat. 12:12), a combination of dumbness, deafness, and fits (Mark 9:17–18, 25), and powers of divination (Acts 16:16). Jesus was able to rebuke these spirits and cast them out (Mark 1:23–26, 5:1–13, etc.). He empowered his disciples to do the same (Mark 3:14–15, Acts 16:16–18, etc.).

There are several related difficulties here. First, the New Testament gives the impression that demon-possession was a common condition – among Jews (Mark 1:32–34, etc.), Samaritans (Acts 8:5–7), and Greeks (Acts 19:11–12). Second, modern medicine attributes dumbness, deafness, blindness, fits, and insanity to physiological or psychological causes. Third, there was a general belief in the 1st century that many disorders are caused by demons.[165] The New Testament seems to follow this.

---

[164] Variously described as *pneuma akatharton* ('unclean spirit'), *pneuma ponēron* ('evil spirit'), and *daimonion* ('demon'). Also *pneuma puthōnalos* (Acts 16:16), after *Puthōn* ('Python'), the serpent slain by Apollo in Greek myth.

[165] See, e.g., Josephus, *Jewish War* 7:185, *Jewish Antiquities* 8:45–49 (Josephus goes beyond the Old Testament account of Solomon here). Cf. Luke 11:19, Acts 19:13–14.

Scholars have sought to resolve these difficulties in several ways.[166] One solution is to note, firstly, that the New Testament does not attribute *all* cases of dumbness, deafness, blindness, fits, and insanity to demons. The New Testament distinguishes between demon-possession and sickness (Mark 1:32–34, etc.). While Jesus rebuked demons and cast them out (Mark 1:23–26, etc.), he generally laid his hands on the sick, or anointed them (Mark 1:40–42, etc.).[167] By this criterion, he treated at least one case of deafness and stuttering as sickness (Mark 7:31–37). He likewise treated most cases of blindness as sickness (Mat. 9:27–31, 20:30–34; Mark 8:22–26; John 9:1–7). He seems also to have treated most people with epilepsy or intermittent insanity as sick (Mat. 4:24).[168] The distinction between these cases and those involving demons seems to have been that demons recognized Jesus and reacted to him (Mark 1:23–24, 32–34; 5:6–8, etc.). They likewise recognized his disciples (Acts 16:16–18, 19:11–17).

Secondly, demon-possession presumably arises when people seek, or are subjected to evil or occult influences, especially when their minds are weak. In the 1st century these influences included pagan gods (1 Cor. 10:20). Jews as well as pagans had a fascination with such gods

---

[166] See, e.g.. Wm. Menzies Alexander, *Demon Possession in the New Testament* (Edinburgh: T. and T. Clark, 1902); Vernon S. McCasland, *By the Finger of God: Demon Possession and Exorcism in Early Christianity in the Light of Modern Views of Mental Illness* (New York: Macmillan, 1951); J.S. Wright, 'Possession', *NBD*; Merrill F. Unger, *Demons in the World Today* (Wheaton: Tyndale House, 1971); John Richards, *But Deliver Us from Evil: An Introduction to the Demonic Dimension in Pastoral Care* (London: Darton, Longman and Todd, 1974); John Warwick Montgomery (ed.), *Demon Possession* (Minneapolis: Bethany House, 1976). See also Davidson Razafiarivony, 'Deliverance from demon possession in the gospels: a study into its backgrounds and application in the church,' *JBT* 3 (2010), 26–41.

[167] A partial exception is his rebuke of a fever (Luke 4:38–39), but in other respects he treated this as an illness (Mat. 8:14–15, Mark 1:29–31).

[168] Based on Matthew's distinction in 4:24 between *diamonizomenous* ('demon-possessed') and *selēniazomenous* (lit. 'moonstruck', i.e. struck intermittently according to phases of the moon). Later Greek writers identify *selēniasmos* with *epilēpsials*, but this may have been under the influence of Matthew's use in 17:15. Latin translators rendered *selēniazomenous* as *lunaticos* (Vulgate). A broad meaning is likely, embracing all disorders involving intermittent strange behaviour.

(cf. Psa. 106:37–38, etc.). A pre-Christian writer explained that evil spirits 'harm men and lead them astray, to sacrifice to demons as to gods'.[169] Demon-possession could therefore have been relatively common in the 1st century.

Thirdly, the gospel-writers may well have drawn particular attention to cases of demon-possession to show that Jesus had power even over demons (Mark 1:27).

Thus, what the New Testament says about demon-possession can be reconciled with modern science if it is accepted that God allows the Devil to work through evil spirits among those who seek them, and that these spirits can produce similar symptoms to, or enhance the symptoms of, natural disorders. Authentic exorcism of a demon (as opposed to human or Satanic counterfeit) requires God's intervention; it was in this connection that Jesus spoke of the Holy Spirit as 'the finger of God' (Mat. 12:28/Luke 11:20).

Demon-possession could become common again as more people engage in occult practices and the worship of Satan. Christian ministers need to be able to distinguish between this and ordinary illness and behavioural disorders. Demon-possession cannot be relieved by medicine or counselling. On the other hand, exorcism should not be used for ordinary physiological or psychological conditions. Diagnosis of a demon and attempted exorcism only confuse the sufferer, and add to his or her troubles. Several authorities have listed signs of demonic attack.[170] I am not competent to comment on these, except to note the Biblical test (reaction to Jesus) referred to above.

---

[169] 1 Enoch 19:1 [Matthew Black, *The Book of Enoch or 1 Enoch* (Leiden: Brill, 1985), 36].

[170] For a compilation, see Richards, *But Deliver Us from Evil*, 155–9.

CHAPTER 9

Another Look at the Genesis Flood

The great flood in Genesis 6–9 is a puzzle. The author describes it as having taken place in history but fitting it into history is very difficult. Scholars have suggested many different ways of doing this, from identifying it with a major flood in Mesopotamia, to making it responsible for most of the sedimentary rocks in the earth's crust.[171] Here I take another look at the problem.[172]

Type of flood

According to Genesis, the waters of the Flood rose and then receded. This immediately eliminates some of the identifications scholars have suggested, e.g. with a surge in the flooding that led to the formation of the Persian Gulf when sea levels rose after the last Ice

---

[171] See, e.g., John C. Whitcomb, Jr., and Henry M. Morris, *The Genesis Flood* (Philadelphia: Presbyterian and Reformed, 1961); Lloyd R. Bailey, *Noah* (University of South Carolina Press, 1989); Davis A. Young, *The Biblical Flood* (Grand Rapids: Eerdmans / Carlisle: Paternoster, 1995); William Ryan and Walter Pitman, *Noah's Flood* (New York: Simon and Schuster, 1999); Robert M. Best, *Noah's Ark and the Ziusudra Epic* (Fort Myers, Florida: Enil Press, 1999); Carol A. Hill, 'A time and a place for Noah,' *Perspectives on Science and Christian Faith* 53 (2001), 24–40, and other articles; Paul H. Seely, 'Noah's flood: its date, extent, and divine accommodation,' *WJT* 66 (2004), 291–311.

[172] Cf. *Big Bang, Small Voice*, Chap. 5.

Age,[173] or with a rapid expansion of the Black Sea through a breach of the Bosporus.[174] It also rules out a *natural* global flood.

Extent of flood

According to Genesis, God 'saw that the evil of mankind[175] was great on the land-area (*'erets*)' (6:5) and said, 'I will wipe out mankind whom I have created from the face of the land-area ...' (6:7). He told Noah, 'I will bring a flood of waters upon the land-area to destroy all flesh in which there is the breath of life from under the heavens' (6:17). The resulting flood extended over 'the face of all the land-area' (8:9).

Here I have tried to capture the general sense of the word *'erets*. In Genesis 1–11, the author uses it to refer to land as opposed to sky (1:1) or seas (1:10), to a particular land (2:11–13 etc.), and to the land area occupied by Noah's descendants after their dispersal (10:32, 11:8–9).[176] He also uses it of the 'world' of Noah's descendants (11:1, 9a). In his account of the Flood, he does not specify a particular land, so he must be referring to land more generally.

The author also says that the floodwaters at their height covered 'all the high peaks (*harim*) under all the heavens' (7:19–20). Here I have tried to capture the general sense of the word *har*, which can refer to a hill or a mountain.[177]

The land area in the narrative includes 'the peaks of Ararat' (8:4). Scholars identify these as mountains north of Mesopotamia, on the plateau that runs from modern Turkey through Armenia to Iran. The highest of these, modern Mount Ararat, is 5,200 metres or 17,000 feet

---

[173] Walter S. Olson, 'Has science dated the Biblical flood?' *Zygon* 2 (1967), 272–8; Bailey, *Noah*, 40–5; J.T. Teller, K.W. Glennie, N. Lancaster, and A.K. Singhvi, 'Calcareous dunes of the United Arab Emirates and Noah's flood: the Postglacial reflooding of the Persian (Arabian) Gulf,' *Quaternary International* 68–71 (2000) 297–308.

[174] Ryan and Pitman, *Noah's Flood*.

[175] Heb. *hā'ādām*, here collective.

[176] The resulting peoples are listed in 10:2–31. Many cannot be identified with any certainty (see commentaries). Those that can occupied an area encompassing the Eastern Mediterranean and Middle East.

[177] See lexicons.

above sea level. Thus if 'all the high peaks' were covered, the greater part of the earth as we know it today must have been covered.

For the Flood to have been on this scale, God would have had to have acted supernaturally. This he could have done. There is still, however, a problem. This is that Noah would have had to have taken on the ark animals from distant parts of the earth. Now he could certainly have done this if God brought these animals to him supernaturally, but then we would have expected him to report that animals came to him that he had not seen before.

A further problem is that there is no archaeological evidence that the ancient world was ever completely flooded. There is evidence of flooding, but only in localized areas.[178]

A possible solution to these problems lies in the conception the ancient Hebrews may have had of the universe. Some references in the Old Testament suggest that they might have thought of the sky as being a solid dome, which rested on the distant mountains of the land area they knew. Thus the author of Genesis describes the sky as a *raqia‘* (1:6–8), a term derived from a verb meaning 'to beat, stamp, or spread', and used of the working of metals.[179] Elihu asks Job, 'Can you, like him, spread out the heavens, strong as a cast metal mirror?' (Job 37:18). Further, David speaks of 'the foundations of the heavens' (2 Sam. 22:8), and Job of 'the pillars of the heavens' (Job 26:11), which may refer to distant mountains.

These references may all, of course, be figurative or poetic. We speak of a 'cloudburst' even though we do not believe that clouds are balloons of water. However, if Noah did have such a conception of the world, then when he said that 'all the high peaks' were covered, he might have excluded the distant mountains. If these included the higher mountains of Ararat, the flood waters would not have been as deep, and would have been confined to a smaller area.

---

[178] For details, see later.
[179] Derek Kidner, *Genesis* (London: Tyndale, 1967), 47.

Some support for this interpretation is provided by the description of the Flood given by the Jewish philosopher Philo of Alexandria, writing in the first century AD. He visualized the Flood as covering all the mountains within the world as he knew it, but not those on the edge of it:[180]

> ... the flood was not a trifling outpouring of water but a limitless and immense one, which almost flowed out beyond the Pillars of Hercules and the Great Sea. Therefore, the whole earth and the mountainous regions were flooded.

The Pillars of Hercules are the rocks on either side of the Strait of Gibraltar.

Where?

If the Flood was confined to the land area known to Noah, where was this?

Genesis gives the impression that the first human population lived around Eden (2:8) and remained in the same general area until the Flood. The author does not refer to the dispersal of populations until after the Flood (Chapters 10–11). Cain settled east of Eden (4:16), but Noah knew enough about his descendants to preserve their history (4:17–24). Jabel's family were nomads (4:20), but there is no reference to any group moving permanently out of the area. If they did, Noah seems not to have known about them.[181]

The author says that Eden was 'in the east' (2:8). Commentators are generally agreed that this means 'east of the land of Canaan'. This points to Mesopotamia as a possible location. Mesopotamia, however, is not mentioned until Chapters 10–11 ('Shinar').

The author also gives the location as the area in which the rivers Pishon, Gihon, Hiddekel (Tigris), and Perath (Euphrates) have their

---

[180] *Questions and Answers on Genesis* 2:28 (Loeb edn., tr. Ralph Marcus). (Marcus identifies the Great Sea as the Atlantic, but it usually refers to the Mediterranean.)
[181] I discuss this further later.

headwaters (2:10-14). The first two rivers cannot be identified, but the Tigris and Euphrates have their headwaters in the highlands north of Mesopotamia, on the Turkish-Iranian plateau. However, Havilah and Cush, the countries around which the author says the Pishon and Gihon flow, are identified elsewhere in the Old Testament as, respectively, Arabia (Gen. 25:18) and Ethiopia (Ezek. 29:10), south of Mesopotamia.

A reasonable solution to this problem is to focus on the Tigris and Euphrates, whose identification is certain. Anyone knowing these rivers would have at least a general idea of where they flowed from. This places Eden on the highland plateau north of Mesopotamia. The Pishon and the Gihon are then two of the other rivers that have their headwaters in this area, and Havilah and Cush are different from Havilah and Cush elsewhere in the Old Testament. Slight support for this is that Havilah and Cush are descriptive names ('swirling or sandy' and 'dark' respectively[182]), which could have been applied to more than one land. Also, *hawilah* carries the definite article in 2:11 (*hahawilah*) but not elsewhere.

Some commentators try to resolve the puzzle by suggesting that the author is describing the river system in an upstream direction.[183] They identify the river in Eden as the Persian Gulf, the 'heads' as river mouths, and the direction of flow as that of an incoming tide. The Assyrians called the Gulf a river (*nar marratum*, 'bitter river'), and the Sumerians apparently thought that high water levels in the Tigris and Euphrates came from the Gulf. However, the narrative (lit. 'a river [kept] going out from Eden to water the garden, and from there it divided') describes a river with a continuous (not tidal) flow,[184] and the

---

[182] See lexicons.
[183] E.A. Spieser, 'The rivers of Paradise,' in *Oriental and Biblical Studies*, ed. J.J. Finkelstein and M. Greenberg (Philadelphia: University of Pennsylvania Press, 1967), 23-34; Kidner, *Genesis*, 63-4.
[184] On the wording, see S.R. Driver, *The Book of Genesis*, 14th edn. (London: Methuen, 1943), 39; John D. Currid, *A Study Commentary on Genesis*, Vol. 1, *Genesis 1:1-25:18* (Darlington: Evangelical Press, 2003), 102.

watering of Paradise by a 'bitter' river seems unlikely. If Eden had been in Mesopotamia, the author could surely have said so.

Another possibility is that Genesis describes the geography of Eden before sea levels rose after the last Ice Age and flooded the basin that now forms the Persian Gulf. This basin was watered mainly by the Tigris, Euphrates, Karun, and Wadi Batin Rivers, which came together to form the Ur-Schatt River, now under the sea.[185] The Karun runs down the mountains east of the Tigris, through an area Speiser identified as the Cush of 2:13.[186] The Wadi Batin comes in from Arabia in the west, a country that was noted for its gold and called Havilah in 25:18.[187] The basin was also watered by subterranean aquifers, calling to mind the 'springs of the great deep' in 7:11 and 8:2. The correspondence here with Genesis is very striking, and suggests that the Genesis flood was a temporary deluge of the basin and Tigris/Euphrates valley before the permanent flooding that formed the Gulf. Against this again, however, is the fact that the author describes one river dividing into four, not four rivers converging into one. Tidal flows cannot be invoked in this case since the Tigris, Euphrates, Karun, and Wadi Batin converged above sea level.

This takes us back to the plateau north of Mesopotamia. Bolder scholars have identified the Pishon and the Gihon with particular rivers on this plateau. The most convincing is the identification of the Gihon with the Araxes/Aras, which flows into the Caspian Sea.[188] This river was once called the Gaihun. Also, $b^e d\bar{o}la\d{h}$ and $š\bar{o}ham$ in 2:12 (LXX *anthrax* and *prasinos*) could refer respectively to obsidian and jadeite, which are found, along with gold, on the plateau.[189]

---

[185] Jeffrey I. Rose, 'New light on human prehistory in the Arabo-Persian Gulf oasis,' *Current Anthropology* 51 (2010), 849–83.
[186] 'The rivers of Paradise,' 25–6.
[187] Wenham, *Genesis 1–15*, 65.
[188] See David M. Rohl, *A Test of Time*, Vol. 2, *Legend* (London: Century, 1998), Chap. 1.
[189] James Mellaart, *The Neolithic of the Near East* (London: Thames and Hudson, 1975), *passim*.

Further support for locating Eden on the plateau is the evidence archaeologists have that human beings began to cultivate cereals, domesticate animals, and work native metals, in the highlands north of Mesopotamia, on the plateau.[190] Here wild forms of rye, wheat, and barley grow, there are wild sheep and goats, and copper and meteoritic iron occur naturally. The author of Genesis gives the impression that these activities originated in and around Eden (3:23; 4:1–2, 20–22).[191]

There is, of course, no river on the plateau that divides into the Tigris, Euphrates, and two other rivers. All the main rivers have separate sources. These do, however, lie in the same general region, along with the mountains of Ararat. It is possible, therefore, that Noah's world lay somewhere in this region,[192] with peaks rising within it, and more distant peaks around it.

Rain on the plateau for 'forty days and forty nights' (Gen.7:12) would have caused widespread flooding. If rivers became dammed, a large area could have been covered. Areas around the plateau could also have been hit. Even where waters did not accumulate, there could still have been loss of life.

When?

A date for the Flood can be calculated from the genealogy in Genesis 11 and other data in the Old Testament. The calculation assumes that the genealogy is complete and that the numbers in it are real.[193] Ussher obtained 2349 BC in this way. Driver revised his

---

[190] Mellaart, *Neolithic of the Near East*; Daniel Zohary and Maria Hopf, *Domestication of Plants in the Old World*, 2nd edn. (Oxford University Press, 1993); David R. Harris (ed.), *The Origins and Spread of Agriculture and Pastoralism in Eurasia* (London: UCL Press, 1996). Metals were not yet being smelted.

[191] Genesis 4:22 describes Tubal-Cain as a 'sharpener' (Heb.) or 'hammerer' (Gk.) of copper and iron.

[192] This region lies north-east of Canaan, but locating Noah's world in this direction does not contradict Genesis 2:8 since in Genesis this bearing is still called 'east' (see 29:1 referring to the people living around Haran, NE of Canaan).

[193] Some scholars think that the numbers in the Genesis genealogies are symbolic, but this is doubtful [see my note, 'Numerology in Genesis,' *Perspectives on Science and Christian Faith* 60 (2008), 70–1]. Many of the numbers could be

calculations and obtained 2501, 2936, or 3066 BC depending on the version (Hebrew, Samaritan, or Greek respectively).[194] The same calculations gave 1491 BC for the date of the Exodus.

Driver, however, calculated the date of the Exodus from Egyptian historical data to be about 1230 BC. Scholars are divided over whether the earlier or the later date is correct.[195] The later date gives about 2240, 2675, or 2805 BC for the Flood.

Radiocarbon dating does not help.[196] If the proportion of radiocarbon in the atmosphere is set equal to the present-day value, the dates obtained agree with those derived from Egyptian historical data by conventional methods. When, however, dates are calibrated by matching and counting tree rings (dendrochronology), significantly earlier dates are obtained (about 300 years earlier at the time of the Exodus). This supports the Biblical dating, but creates problems for Egyptologists, especially for those who think that even the conventional historical dates are too early.[197]

Because of this, I shall in the following discussion give two dates for events. The later one will be the conventional historical date or an uncalibrated radiocarbon date; the earlier one will be a calibrated radiocarbon date or the conventional historical date adjusted to be consistent with calibrated radiocarbon dates.[198] This avoids the

---

rounded, hence the non-random distribution of last digits [cf. Carol A. Hill, 'Response to P.G. Nelson's "Numerology in Genesis",' *ibid.* 60 (2008), 144]. If numbers ending in 0 and 5 are omitted, the chances of the remaining numbers ending with the digits they do are relatively high (one in only 4^5 in the case considered by Hill).

[194] Driver, *Genesis*, xxv–xxxi.
[195] K.A. Kitchen, *Ancient Orient and Old Testament* (London: Tyndale, 1966), *On the Reliability of the Old Testament* (Grand Rapids: Eerdmans, 2003); David M. Rohl, *A Test of Time*, Vol. 1 (London: Century, 1995).
[196] See *Big Bang, Small Voice*, 65–7.
[197] See, e.g., Rohl, *A Test of Time*, Vol. 1, App. C. For a review of chronologies based on historical data, see John Bimson, *(When) Did It Happen?* (Cambridge: Grove, 2003).
[198] In this update, I have used the calibration at http://c14.arch.ox.ac.uk/intcal09.14c. I have rounded very approximate dates.

problem of inadvertently comparing dates on different scales. The dates in bold print are those given by authors.

Now a problem with all of the above dates for the Flood is that they fall in a period of history when a wide area of the ancient world was known, and no flooding of the whole area took place. There were repeated floods in Mesopotamia, including one that left deposits of clay at Shuruppak and Kish in about 3600/**2900** BC, near to the Biblical date.[199] There are also flood stories from the area, and a reference to a flood in a king list.[200] However, there are no signs of a widespread flood (a layer of clay or, where clay has been washed away, a break in culture) in the Middle East at this time.[201] The history of Egypt, for example, is unbroken from the beginning of the Naqada period (about **4000**/3300 BC) onwards.[202] The Nile overflowed annually, in some years more than others, but the population was never wiped out.

Many scholars resolve this problem by confining the Flood to Mesopotamia.[203] The flood stories from this area are in some ways very similar to the one in Genesis.[204] A man builds a boat to escape from the

---

[199] M.E.L. Mallowan, 'Noah's flood reconsidered,' *Iraq* 26 (1964), 62–82.

[200] James B. Pritchard (ed.), *Ancient Near Eastern Texts* (Princeton University Press, 2nd edn., 1955), 42–4, 93–7, 104–6, 265–6; André Parrot, *The Flood and Noah's Ark* (tr. Edwin Hudson; London: SCM Press, 1955), 22–37, 41–42; Samuel Noah Kramer, 'Reflections on the Mesopotamian flood: the cuneiform data new and old,' *Expedition* 9, No.4 (1967), 12–8; Irving Finkel, *The Ark before Noah: Decoding the Story of the Flood* (London: Hodder and Stoughton, 2014). [The fragment described by H.V. Hilprecht, *The Earliest Version of the Babylonian Deluge Story and the Temple Library of Nippur* (Philadelphia: University of Pennsylvania, 1910), is translated differently and dated later by George A. Barton, 'Hilprecht's fragment of the Babylonian deluge story,' *Journal of the American Oriental Society* 31 (1911) 30–48, and corresponds to Finkel's 'Middle Babylonian Nippur' (*op. cit.*, 96).]

[201] See James Mellaart, *Earliest Civilizations of the Near East* (London: Thames and Hudson, 1965), 12; Seely, 'Noah's flood,' 299–301.

[202] Stephen Quirke and Jeffrey Spencer (eds.), *The British Museum Book of Ancient Egypt* (London: British Museum Press, 1992).

[203] Among recent authors, Best, *Noah's Ark and the Ziusudra Epic*; Hill, 'A time and a place for Noah,' and other articles; Seely, 'Noah's flood.'

[204] See Pritchard, *Ancient Near Eastern Texts*, 42–4, 93–7, 104–6; Parrot, *The Flood and Noah's Ark*, 22–37; Kramer, 'Reflections on the Mesopotamian flood'; Finkel, *The Ark before Noah*.

flood, and takes on to it his family and animals ('two by two'). When the flood subsides, he sends out birds to see whether they return. However, there are also big differences. Besides the polytheism in the stories, the floodwaters take only seven days to rise, and seven or so days to fall (the Genesis flood lasted over a year). The boat has a different shape (circular or cubic), and grounds on 'Mount Nisir/Nimush', identified as a peak on the Turkish-Iranian plateau *east of* Mesopotamia.[205] The hero's descendants do not go on to become the nations listed in Genesis 10, some of which already existed in 3600/2900 BC [e.g. Mizraim (Egypt)]. The two events were evidently therefore different. If the Flood had been in Mesopotamia, the author could have stated this, as in 11:2.

Paul Seely resolves this problem by suggesting that the author of Genesis wrote about the Flood as having been bigger than it was because this is how people thought about it at the time.[206] He attributes this to divine accommodation. Dr. Arthur G. Fraser has suggested to me that God wanted the Flood to be seen as an eschatological event like events in the book of Revelation (cf. 2 Pet. 3:3–7). As we have seen, however, the flood in the Mesopotamian flood stories only lasted two weeks or so. People will therefore have known that it had not been on the scale described in Genesis. Also, the author of Genesis presents the times when different things happened in the Flood very precisely as if Noah kept a log (Gen. 7:11; 8:4, 5, 13, 14).

An alternative approach is to take the genealogy in Genesis 11 as selective, and dating the Flood earlier. Many genealogies in the Bible are selective, and use 'X fathered Y' to mean 'X fathered the line that led to Y'.[207] However, those in Genesis 5 and 11 are exceptional in

---

[205] See Ephraim A. Speiser, 'Southern Kurdistan,' *Annual of the* American *Schools of Oriental Research* 8 (1926/7), 1–42 (17–8). Best thinks the reference is to a sand bank in the Persian Gulf (*Noah's Ark and the Ziusudra Epic*, 277). Finkel thinks the Babylonian map of the world refers to the landing of the boat, and places this in the north east, beyond Mount Ararat (*The Ark before Noah*, Chap. 12). The reference is not, however, definite, and the map looks symbolic.

[206] 'Noah's flood,' 303–11.

[207] Francis A. Schaeffer, *No Final Conflict* (London: Hodder and Stoughton, 1975), Chap. 4.

providing information (the age at which each man fathers a named son) that enables a chronology to be constructed from them if they are complete, but which serves no obvious purpose otherwise.

However, a possible indication that these genealogies are selective is the occurrence of an extra name (Cainan) in the ancient Greek version of Genesis 11 as compared with the Hebrew and the Samaritan version.[208] This could mean that all three versions are shortened versions of a longer one.[209] There is also a comment by an early Armenian scholar on Noah being the tenth from Adam in Genesis 5: 'Some used to say that there were innumerable aeons from Adam to Noah'.[210] Moses, who compiled Genesis, was brought up in Egypt, and might have known from Egyptian history that there had not been total flooding of Egypt at the genealogical date.

Now there were floods in Mesopotamia before the genealogical date. There was one that left a layer of clay at Ur, which is dated about 4800/**4000** BC, and one that left a layer at Nineveh, dated about 5100/**4300** BC.[211] David Rohl associates the Genesis flood with the first (redating it to 3800/**3100** BC),[212] and Victor Pearce with both (dating them to about **5000/4000** BC).[213] Once again, however, while there may have been flooding elsewhere, there are no signs that this extended right across the ancient world.[214] Seely's suggestion again does not help, because trade routes at this time were well established,[215]

---

[208] Driver, *Genesis*, 138. Luke includes Cainan (3:36).

[209] Jude will have used a standard version in Jude 14.

[210] Insertion in Philo's *Questions and Answers on Genesis* 1.87 (Loeb edn., 55, note i).

[211] William H. Stiebing, Jr., 'A futile quest: the search for Noah's ark,' *The Biblical Archaeology Review* 2, No. 2 (1976), 1, 13–20. I am very grateful to Carol Hill for this reference.

[212] Rohl, *Test of Time*, Vol. 2, Chap. 5.

[213] E.K. Victor Pearce, *Who Was Adam?* 3rd edn. (Walkerville, South Africa: Africa Centre for World Mission, 1987), Chap. 9; *Evidence for Truth*, Vol. 1 (Eastbourne: Evidence Programmes, 1993), Chaps. 12–5.

[214] See Mellaart, *Earliest Civilizations of the Near East*, 12; Seely, 'Noah's flood,' 299–301.

[215] Mellaart, *Neolithic of the Near East*, 9, 40–1.

and people will have known that the flood did not affect neighbouring areas.

This suggests that the Flood was earlier than 5000/4000 BC. This is supported by the movement of population described in Genesis. As we have seen, the author gives the impression that Noah's world was the area around Eden, which we have located on the plateau north of Mesopotamia. Then came the Flood, and the grounding of the ark on 'the peaks of Ararat' (8:4), in the same general region. After this, Noah's descendants became the various nations known to the ancient Hebrews (10:1–32). The author explains that they 'journeyed in the east [i.e. east of the land of Canaan]' and 'found a plain in the land of Shinar [Mesopotamia], and dwelt there' (11:1–2). In Shinar, they built a city, with a very high tower (11:3–4). God responded to this display of human arrogance by confusing their language and scattering them (11:5–9).

Now there is archaeological evidence for the movement of population from the Turkish-Iranian plateau on to the Mesopotamian plain.[216] Archaeologists date this to **6000/5000–4000**/3300 BC. This dates the Flood to before (6000/5000 + x) BC, where x is the time it took for Noah's family after the Flood to build up to the population that moved into Mesopotamia. If x was about 500 years, this dates the Flood to before about 6500/5500 BC.

At one time, archaeologists thought there were breaks in occupation at sites in the Middle East around 8300/**7300** and 6900/**6000** BC, the latter being attributed to a reduction in rainfall.[217,218] According

---

[216] Geoffrey Barraclough and Geoffrey Parker, *The Times Atlas of World History*, 4th edn. (London: Times Books, 1993), 40–1.
[217] Charles Keith Maisels, *The Emergence of Civilization* (London and New York: Routledge, 1990), 82.
[218] Patrick O'Connell arrived at a date of **7000**/6000 BC for the Flood, but by conflating evidence of flooding in the ancient world [*Science of To-day and the Problems of Genesis* (Minnesota: Radio Replies Press Society, 1959), Book II, Part I]. On his explanation of the salt desert ('Great Kavir') on the Iranian plateau (57–9), compare M.H. Ganji, 'Post-Glacial climatic changes on the Iranian plateau,' in William C. Brice (ed.), *The Environmental History of the*

to recent work, however, there are no signs of contemporaneous breaks back to **12,300**/10,300 BC.²¹⁹ Abu Hureyra, on the upper Euphrates, was continuously occupied from 11,500/**9500** to 6000/**5000** BC.²²⁰

This means that the Flood took place before 12,300/10,300 BC. This takes us back to a time before there is evidence of trade around the Middle East (9000/8000 BC).²²¹ This suggests that Noah's world was relatively small. This correlates with the impression Genesis gives that Noah's world was confined to the area around Eden, which we have located on the Turkish-Iranian plateau. This points to the Flood being confined to a relatively small area, somewhere in this region, sometime before the above date.

How long before is difficult to establish. According to Pearce,²²² there is a break at sites in the Middle East between about 13,000/**11,000** and 11,000/**9000** BC, but this is based on old data.²²³ Archaeological sites on the plateau are sparse.²²⁴ In the discussion above, we supposed that it would take about 500 years for the human population to build up again after the Flood. This would date the Flood to before about 12,800/10,800 BC.

A problem with a date as early as this is that human culture at this time was less advanced than it was in the time of Noah. As we have seen, Genesis describes human beings before the Flood cultivating the ground, keeping flocks, and working metals (4:1–2, 20–22).²²⁵ The

---

Near and Middle East since the Last Ice Age (London: Academic Press, 1978), Chap. 10.

²¹⁹ Steven Mithen, *After the Ice: a Global Human History 20,000–5000 BC* (London: Weidenfeld and Nicolson, 2003), Chaps. 3–11; Seely, 'Noah's flood,' 301–2. Note that Seely's dates for Abu Hureyra are uncalibrated.

²²⁰ A.M.T. Moore, G.C. Hillman, and A.J. Legge, *Village on the Euphrates: from Foraging to Farming at Abu Hureyra* (Oxford: Oxford University Press, 2000).

²²¹ Mellaart, *Neolithic of the Near East*, 9, 40–1. The earliest trade was in obsidian, a dark volcanic rock found on the Turkish-Iranian plateau.

²²² Pearce, *Who Was Adam?*, 83.

²²³ Cf. Mithen, *After the Ice*.

²²⁴ *Ibid.*

²²⁵ Pearce thinks that the building of cities also came before the Flood (*Who Was Adam?*, 78). He bases this on the RSV of 4:17, 'Cain built a city' (48). However, the Hebrew term '*îr* denotes a settlement of any size. Seely ('Noah's

earliest archaeological evidence for these activities is dated 11,000/**9000** BC (agriculture),[226] 9000/**7500** BC (pasturing),[227] and 9000/**7500** BC (metalworking).[228]

We must remember, however, that the world Noah knew was confined to the area around Eden. Farming and metalworking could thus have been limited to where he lived and not practised elsewhere. Also, any remains could have been destroyed in the Flood.

We must remember too that there were only eight human beings on the ark (7:13). The human population would therefore have taken a long time to build up again.[229] Also, not all of Noah's descendants may have taken up farming and metalworking after the Flood, but may have opted to gather and hunt. The culture that existed in Noah's world before the Flood could therefore have taken many years to become re-established and leave remains. This may also explain the gap between Noah planting a vineyard (Gen. 9:20) and the earliest evidence of viticulture (7000/**6000** BC).[230]

These considerations nevertheless suggest that the Flood will not have been very much earlier than 12,800/10,800 BC. My tentative conclusion, therefore, is that the Flood took place around 13,000/11,000 BC, on the Turkish-Iranian plateau, north of Mesopotamia. This early date stretches the genealogy of Genesis 11, but keeping to the genealogical date is very difficult as we have seen. At least the early date explains how the author of Genesis could

---

flood', 291–2) suggests that the Flood took place after the domestication of fruit trees (about **4000**/3300 BC) because of the fruit trees in Genesis 2–3. However, these had been planted by God (2:8–9). Adam's punishment was to eat the plants of the field (3:17–19).

[226] Moore et al., *Village on the Euphrates*, 478, 9.
[227] *Ibid.*, 478.
[228] Mellaart, *Neolithic of the Near East*, 52–4.
[229] A population of eight doubling in size every 30 years would take 500 years to reach one million.
[230] Patrick E. McGovern, Ulrich Hartung, Virginia R. Badler, Donald L. Glusker, and Lawrence J. Exner, 'The beginnings of winemaking and viniculture in the ancient Near East and Egypt,' *Expedition* 39, No. 1 (1997), 3–21; Rod Phillips, *A Short History of Wine* (London: Penguin, 2000), Chap.1.

describe the Flood as covering 'the face of all the *'erets'*: it *was* 'all the *'erets'* known to Noah.

The early date for the Flood means that the flooding in Mesopotamia that gave rise to flood stories similar to the one in Genesis was much later. The reason for the similarity may be that the hero had some knowledge of Noah, and followed his example.

The ark

There is indirect evidence for the use of boats at the above date for the Flood.[231] Possible remains of boats have been found by the Persian Gulf dating from about **6000**/5000 BC, and in the upper Euphrates valley dated **3800**/3100 BC.[232]

According to Genesis, God told Noah to make the ark of *gopher* wood and cover it with *kopher* (6:14). These terms are used only here in the Old Testament. This is consistent with placing Noah on the edge of the Old Testament world. *Kopher* would have been some form of bitumen, sources of which occur all over the Middle East, including the Turkish-Iranian plateau.[233] The ark was remarkably large (6:15), even by later standards.

Discussion

Christians who believe that the Flood was global, and caused the formation of most of the sedimentary rocks in the earth's crust, will be disappointed by my conclusion. Let me say at once, therefore, that it is still possible to explain the formation of these rocks within a literal understanding of Genesis, as I showed in Chapter 2.

There are in any case problems with the idea that most sedimentary rocks were formed in the Flood. Quite apart from the

---

[231] Seán McGrail, *Boats of the World: from the Stone Age to Medieval Times*, paperback edn. (Oxford University Press, 2004), vii–viii.

[232] *Ibid.*, viii–ix.

[233] Z.R. Beydoun, 'Prehistoric, ancient and mediaeval occurrences and uses of hydrocarbons in the greater Middle East region,' *Journal of Petroleum Geology* 20 (1997), 91–5.

geological difficulties,[234] the author of Genesis describes the rivers in Eden before the Flood as if his readers knew them (2:10–14). Today the Tigris and Euphrates flow through the Mesopotamian plain over layers of sedimentary rock thousands of feet thick.[235] Before these were laid, the rivers in the region would have been very different. Further, Noah correctly anticipated that a dove would find olive trees growing after the waters had subsided (8:8–11). There could not therefore have been a major reworking of the earth's crust in the Flood.

If anthropologists are right that, by 13,000/11,000 BC, *Homo sapiens* had colonized most of the earth,[236] the human world in Noah's time was much wider than he knew. This does not mean, however, that the Flood does not have a wider significance. What happened in the Flood seems to have been played out, at different times, in various parts of the world. There are an extraordinary number of flood stories from all over the globe.[237] Major flooding was doubtless a common phenomenon at the end of the last Ice Age. To this extent, the Genesis flood is a 'type' of all the others, in showing God's wrath at the behaviour of his creatures, while preserving a few to allow them to continue. Noah is picked out because he fathered the line that led to Abraham and the nation of Israel, from which would come the Messiah and 'Light of the World'.

---

[234] See, e.g., Young, *The Biblical Flood*.
[235] See Carol A. Hill, 'The Garden of Eden: a modern landscape,' *Perspectives on Science and Christian Faith* 52 (2000), 31–46, Fig. 3. (Her location of Eden is different from mine.)
[236] See, e.g., Mithen, *After the Ice*.
[237] Bernhard Lang, 'Non-Semitic deluge stories and the book of Genesis: a bibliographical and critical survey,' *Anthropos* 80 (1985), 605–16.

CHAPTER 10

What Will Happen in the End Times

Theologians differ widely in their understanding of what will happen in the end times.[238] The difficulty is knowing how to interpret the various scriptures on this, especially in the book of Revelation, and how to bring them together. In this note, I present one way of doing this for readers for whom eschatology is a problem.

First, I need to consider what happens when we die, and discuss the symbolism in the book of Revelation.

Death

Some theologians believe that, when we die, we simply fall asleep. This is the language Paul uses (Acts 13:36; 1 Cor. 11:30; 15:6, 18, 20, 51; 1 Thes. 4:13–15), but I take this to be euphemistic, as Jesus made clear when he used it (John 11:11–15). I accordingly suppose that the soul or spirit of a person lives on after the death of the body (Luke 23:39–43, Heb. 12:22–24, Rev. 6:9–11). Resurrection then involves raising the body and reuniting it with the soul or spirit.

According to Jesus, the souls of the dead before he came were in different places – the righteous in Abraham's bosom and the unrighteous in a place of torment (Luke 16:19–31). The writer to the Hebrews indicates that, as a result of Jesus coming and securing the 'perfection' of the righteous, the spirits of the righteous dead are now in heaven (Heb. 11:39–40, 12:22–24). This differentiation between the

---

[238] See, e.g., J. Daniel Hays, J. Scott Duvall, and C. Marvin Pate, *Dictionary of Biblical Prophecy and End Times* (Grand Rapids: Zondervan, 2007).

righteous and the unrighteous implies a judgment at death (Heb. 9:27), of which the Last Judgment is a public confirmation.

Symbolism in the book of Revelation

The book of Revelation comprises a series of visions John had when he was imprisoned for his faith on the island of Patmos. These visions are highly symbolic. In some places, this is stated (e.g. Rev. 1:20). In other places, the symbolism is apparent from the nature of what John sees. For example, he sees the New Jerusalem as a cube, 1,400 miles long, 1,400 miles wide, and 1,400 miles *high* (Rev. 21:16). This is extraordinary. Again, he sees each of the twelve gates of the city as being made of a single pearl (Rev. 21:21). This again is extraordinary.

In the first case, the significance of the symbolism is easy to see. The shape of the city is the same as that of the inner sanctuary in the Tabernacle and Temple (Exod. 26:31–34,[239] 1 Kgs. 6:20). This is where God dwelt with his people. John sees the New Jerusalem as the place where God will dwell with his people (Rev. 21:22).

In the second case, the significance of the symbolism is less clear. Is it simply that the splendour of the New Jerusalem will be out of the ordinary (cf. Isa. 54:11–12), or does it have some other significance?

What all this means is that we must not interpret John's visions too literally, but be prepared to encounter symbolism in them.

What will happen?

I suggest that what will happen in the end times is the following.

• Jesus will come again (Acts 2:10–11[240]).

---

[239] Scholars believe that the curtain described in these verses made the Most Holy Place a cube.

[240] Here I take this to refer to Jesus' coming again in the end times. For other references, see my article, 'What Jesus said about coming again', *JBT* 2(1) (2019) 153–72.

- He will judge the living and assign the righteous to eternal life and the unrighteous to eternal punishment (Mat. 25:31–46).

- He will cast the unrighteous, and their leaders, into a 'lake of fire' (Rev. 19:11–21).

- He will make Satan suffer the internment he made Christians suffer (Rev. 20:1–3) and then cast him also into the 'lake of fire' (Rev. 20:7–10). The internment will be for a 'thousand years'.

- He will reward the martyrs by raising them from the dead to witness the punishment of Satan and to reign with Jesus (Rev. 20:4–6).[241]

- He will raise the remaining dead, judge them, and cast the unrighteous into the 'lake of fire' (Dan. 12:1–4, John 5:25–29, Mat. 25:31–46,[242] Rev. 20:11–15).

- He will give the righteous, living and dead, new bodies (1 Cor. 15, 1 Thes. 4:13–18).

- He will usher in a new heaven and a new earth for the righteous to live in (Rev. 21:1–22:5).

In the above, the 'lake of fire' and the 'thousand years' could be symbolic. Being cast into a 'lake of fire' could symbolize the eternal punishment Jesus spoke about (Mat. 25:46), and internment for a 'thousand years' could symbolize total disempowerment, something Satan would hate.

This scheme is premillennialist, but with the possibility of a symbolic millennium.

---

[241] Reading verse 4, 'And I saw thrones, and they sat on them, and judgment was given to them, namely [epexegetic *kai*] the souls of those who had been axed because of the witness of Jesus and because of the word of God, and who did not worship the beast ...'. See my article, 'Why the millennium?', *AJBT* 21(1) (2020).

[242] I presume that, when Jesus says he will judge 'all the nations', he includes the dead, as he did on other occasions he referred to the Day of Judgment (Mat. 10:11–15, 11:20–24, 12:39–42; John 5:25–29).

Epilogue

A long study of God and the universe calls for, at the end, a doxology. Not only has God created a universe containing billions of galaxies each comprising billions of stars, but also a star with a planet on which there are millions of different kinds of living organisms, including one that is capable of wondering at it all and seeking him. What better than the doxology Paul gave at the end of his long discussion of the gospel and of God's dealings in human history (Rom. 11:33–36):[243]

> [33]O [the] depth of [the] riches and wisdom and knowledge of God! How unsearchable [are] his judgments and untraceable his ways! [34]For 'who has known [the] mind of [the] Lord, or who has become his advisor?' [35]Or 'who has first given to him, and he will repay him?' [36]Because from him and through him and to him [are] all things. To him [be] the glory forever. Amen.

---

[243] Verse 34 is from Isa. 40:13 and verse 35 from Job 41:11. Verse 35 is lit., 'and it will be repaid to him'.

Printed in Great Britain
by Amazon